A Practical Legal Guide for Tourists and Business Travelers

Germany

By Michael L. Moore Esq.

DEDICATION

This book is dedicated to the memory of my late older brother, Kenneth Lee Moore, whose tragic murder at 15 years of age inspired me to write this series of books.

This book is also dedicated to my parents, John Henry Moore, and Edna Mae Moore, whose tremendous parenting skills kept me focused on the important things in life: being reverent, getting educated, and prioritizing family.

Finally, this book is dedicated to my beautiful family, my wife Royellen, my son AJ, and my daughter Karla. They inspire me every single day to be kind, patient, and compassionate.

IN LOVING MEMORY OF:

Belinda Joyce Moore Moss—my beautiful and wonderful sister, who supported me in every positive thing that I ever attempted to do.

Michael Eugene Baker—my dedicated and loyal friend and brother, who always wanted the very best for me.

Sylvia Joyce Hill—my eldest sister, who had a beautiful spirit and was like a second mother to me.

LAW OF THE LAND ®

PUBLISHING for Tourists & Business Travelers

Travel smart. Stay legal. Stay safe.®

**From local laws to medical guides
we've got you covered world wide
in one digital platform.**

PREFACE

My introduction to the justice system came when I was only 10 years old. My 15-year-old brother was murdered with a butcher knife by a 19-year-old in a simple argument over a torn shirt. I was devastated by his death and sought retribution for his fate that never came. The woman was initially charged with second degree murder, but after plea negotiations, she was convicted of manslaughter and sentenced to only five years in a youthful offender school and ordered to undergo psychiatric care. That was it. Nothing more. The judicial system had run its course.

My family knew nothing about the justice system, and we did not have the tools to advocate for ourselves. No one provided us with a written source to reference for guidance through this process. There was no easily accessible, easy to understand, definitive source to educate ourselves about the legal system that we suddenly and unexpectedly found ourselves immersed in after being victimized by such a violent criminal act.

As I got older, finished college, law school, and ultimately started practicing law, it became clear to me that most people are not knowledgeable about the law or how the judicial process works. If most people are uninformed here in the United States regarding the law and the legal process, how would they fare when in other countries? I realized that tourists and businesspeople who travel internationally needed access to information on how to navigate the legal system in other countries!

For many years, there has been considerable media attention focused on international travelers experiencing legal difficulties while traveling abroad. Most of these news stories gained attention in the United States and abroad because they involved American citizens facing punishment that was considered "unconventional" and "harsh" by United States' legal standards. I recall a news story in 1994 regarding Michael Fay, a young American male, who had broken the law in Singapore. He was convicted and sentenced to be caned and or whipped publicly. While the United States Government weighed in on the inappropriate and cruel nature of the punishment, the young American was beaten because he had been convicted under Singapore law.

Similarly, in recent years, international news stories have garnered headlines regarding foreign travelers and their issues with the laws of countries that were not their own. Amanda Knox, an American woman, was accused of murdering her roommate in Italy in 2007 and spent almost four years in an Italian prison before being definitively acquitted by the Supreme Court of Cassatio. Kenneth Bae, an American citizen, was arrested in North Korea in 2012 and was convicted for hostile acts against the communist country. He was sentenced to 15 years hard labor but was released in 2014 after efforts by the U.S. State Department. More recently, United States Basketball Star, Brittany Griner was arrested in February 2022 at a Moscow airport on drug-related charges and detained for nearly 10 months, spending much of that time in prison. Her plight unfolded at the same time Russia invaded Ukraine and further heightened tensions between Russia and the United States, ending only after she was freed in exchange for a notorious Russian arms dealer.

It was in 1994 that another personal tragic event occurred that finally inspired me to write these series of books. A dear friend and also client of mine was brutally murdered while on his second honeymoon in Jamaica. News of his murder shocked me and our local community. The legal hurdles his family had to overcome to see that justice was properly dispensed far away from home, in another country, with an entirely different set of criminal procedural rules and laws, was difficult to navigate.

As I was my friend's attorney at the time of his death, his family asked that I act as their "legal liaison" to the Jamaican Prosecutor's Office and to the Jamaican Police Department. I participated in multiple police interviews with my client's widow because she was the primary witness to his murder. As a former prosecuting attorney, I was also allowed by the Court, as a professional courtesy, to sit at the prosecutor's table to consult with the prosecuting attorney during trial. What I observed about the Jamaican trial process from a front row seat was compelling enough to cause me to seriously consider educating the "world" regarding what to expect and how to act appropriately when faced with legal issues while traveling abroad.

One of the realities in life is that, regardless of what country you are in, it is never a pleasant experience to run afoul of the law and be forced to accept that someone else will be making a decision about your pecuniary, proprietary, or penal interests (your money, your property, or your freedom).

It is important to know what the laws are, how they apply to you, and how to navigate the legal system if you are charged with a crime. It is also very helpful to know what resources are available to you if you are the victim of a criminal act. At the end of the day, an "ounce of prevention is worth a pound of cure," so the more knowledge you have, the more ammunition you possess, and the more likely you will have a positive outcome.

If you are traveling to Germany, the first thing you should pack is a copy of this book! The helpful information and tips contained in this volume will provide a great starting point for knowing what to do (and not to do!) when you arrive at your destination and will help ensure that you have a wonderful vacation or business trip unmarred by tangles with the law.

TABLE OF CONTENTS

INTRODUCTION

INTRODUCTION

As a practicing attorney for over 34 years, I have encountered numerous clients who travel often, but are unaware of the laws of the land they are traveling to.

Therefore, many years ago, I decided to write a series of books that would explain the laws of specific countries. My focus was to explain the laws that may affect travelers in a straightforward manner, without all of the legal language that is sometimes hard for even seasoned attorneys to understand.

About This Book

The aim of this book is simple. It provides you, the traveler, with a simple, easy to read book that will provide a basic legal guide that explains the law in the country that you are about to visit. It is not intended to educate you on ALL of the laws in a given country. The goal is to provide you with the details of the most common legal and safety issues faced by tourists and business travelers.

I have also provided context with background information on places not to visit, statistics on the country and prevention measures you should take to safeguard your legal and physical safety. Knowledge is a powerful thing and knowing how to stay out of trouble (or how to get out of it!) is important for everyone who travels.

This *Law of The Land/GERMANY* book simply helps you become more informed about your legal rights, responsibilities, and obligations in a wide range of subject areas.

Last, but not least, this book does NOT purport to offer legal advice. It does, however, provide the information you need to stay safe, follow the law and navigate around legal difficulties. However, if you do face legal difficulties, the information in this book will provide you with a starting point for solving the problem and obtaining legal assistance should it be required.

Hypotheticals Used Throughout This Book

From time to time throughout this book, I will explain the law to readers by using hypothetical scenarios. These hypotheticals will be marked by an icon that will be explained in further detail as you read on.

How This Book is Organized

CHAPTER 1: **About Germany.** This chapter will provide you with a brief overview about Germany and its history. It also addresses Visa requirements, monetary advice, and the best times to visit.

CHAPTER 2: **Customs.** This chapter will provide information on what to expect when entering Germany. It will also explain what restricted and prohibited items are when entering Germany along with custom's regulations.

CHAPTER 3: **Crime in Germany.** This chapter provides an overview of the history of crime in Germany and steps that Germany's officials have taken to curb the high rate of crime.

CHAPTER 4: **Criminal Law Violations.** This chapter will provide information on drug offenses, penalties, true events and questions and answers.

CHAPTER 5: **Alcohol-Related Offenses.** This chapter will provide key points regarding the sale, consumption, and regulations of alcohol use in Germany.

CHAPTER 6: **Firearm & Ammunition Offenses.** This chapter will provide key points regarding the possession of firearms and ammunition in Germany.

CHAPTER 7: **Prostitution.** This chapter provides an overview of the history of prostitution in Germany, laws and penalties, prostitution practices, sex trafficking, sex tourism, health in Germany, tips to avoid being hassled, a Law of the Land Hypothetical, and the current situation on prostitution in Germany.

CHAPTER 8: **LGBTQ.** This chapter will provide information regarding the acceptance of LGBTQ people in Germany and the laws surrounding homosexuality.

CHAPTER 9: **Sexually Motivated/Violent Crimes.** This chapter will provide an overview of sexually related crimes in Germany.

CHAPTER 10: **Arrested in Germany.** This chapter will provide information on what to do if you are arrested in Germany.

CHAPTER 11: **Jails vs. Prisons: Conditions & Culture.** This chapter will provide information on the conditions and culture of Germany's Jails and Prisons.

CHAPTER 12: **Helping a Friend or Relative Imprisoned in Germany.** This chapter will provide information on how you can assist a friend or relative imprisoned in Germany.

CHAPTER 13: **The Administration of Justice.** This chapter will provide information on Germany's Legal System.

CHAPTER 14: **Crime Victim Assistance.** This chapter will provide information on crime victim assistance along with providing safety tips.

CHAPTER 15: **Police.** This chapter will provide information on Germany's Police and how to report a crime.

CHAPTER 16: **How to Get Legal Help in Germany.** This chapter will provide information regarding how to obtain legal assistance for travelers to Germany.

CHAPTER 17: **Medical Facilities & Hospitals.** This chapter will provide information about how to obtain medical care while visiting Germany.

CHAPTER 18: **Driving in Germany.** This chapter will provide information on driving in Germany, it's traffic rules, and road safety tips.

CHAPTER 19: **Nude Beaches & Clothing-Optional Resorts.** This chapter will provide an overview of nude beaches and clothing-optional resorts in Germany, and the legality and safety of visiting nude beaches in Germany.

CHAPTER 20: **Unusual Laws.** This chapter will provide information on some Unusual Laws in Germany, and penalties and fines.

CHAPTER 21: **Traveling Safely.** This chapter will provide information on women traveling alone, crime prevention for families, safety notes for all travelers, and overall advice.

CHAPTER 22: **Tourist Taxation.** This chapter will provide information on taxes that tourists are required to pay in Germany.

CHAPTER 23: **Long-Term Stays.** This chapter will provide an overview of the consequences for overstaying your visit to Germany.

CHAPTER 24: **Civil Litigation.** This chapter will provide information about the civil litigation process in Germany.

CHAPTER 25: **Other Things to Know.** This chapter will provide information on the harassment of tourists, travel and safety, and other practical tips.

CHAPTER 26: **Quick Reference Guide.** This chapter is a quick way to get information. It is a condensed version of the chapters in this book.

Emergency/Important Contact Numbers in Germany

Useful German Phrases

Glossary

Icons Used in this Book

What do those pictures throughout the book mean? See below:

WARNING: This icon flags information about things you should **avoid** while visiting Germany. Heed the advice next to this icon to avoid legal perils.

REMEMBER: This icon flags noteworthy information that you **shouldn't forget**.

HELPFUL TIPS: This icon flags information that will help you when entering Germany, relates to a legal situation, or refers to resources available while visiting Germany.

TECHNICAL INFORMATION: This icon flags technical aspects of the law. If you are faced with a legal problem, and you want to learn more about the law involved, this information can be helpful.

 **ADDITIONAL INFORMATION**: This icon points to the location of additional information available on the internet.

 **HYPOTHETICAL**: This icon points to hypothetical scenarios to illustrate possible legal problems and the outcome.

 **QUESTIONS**: This icon points to questions and answers throughout the book.

 **TRUE STORY**: This icon points to true events throughout the book.

Where to Go From Here

If you have a specific question about the law in Germany as it relates to a particular area, just turn to the chapter that addresses that issue, or turn to the Quick Reference Guide. You can also read the book from cover to cover to obtain a more comprehensive understanding of Germany's laws and resources available should you find yourself in a legal predicament while visiting.

 **Disclaimer:** While the recommendations in this book primarily address U.S. citizens, the information is relevant and applicable to citizens of any country.

ABOUT GERMANY

CHAPTER 1

ABOUT GERMANY

About Germany[1]

Germany, located in Central Europe, is **the largest country in the European Union**, covering an area of approximately 357,022 square kilometers (137,988 square miles). With a population of about **84 million people**, it is one of the most populous nations in Europe. The country shares borders with nine countries, including France, Poland, and Austria. Germany plays a pivotal role on the global stage, boasting the **largest economy in Europe** and the **fourth largest in the world**. It is a leader in industries like automotive manufacturing, engineering, and technology, and has significant influence in international organizations such as the European Union, the United Nations, and NATO. Known for its **political stability**, **economic power**, and **cultural heritage**, Germany holds a prominent position in both European and global affairs.

The country is renowned for its contributions to philosophy, music, and literature, with figures like **Johann Wolfgang von Goethe, Ludwig van Beethoven**, and **Albert Einstein** shaping Western thought and culture. It is also famous for its **engineering excellence**, particularly in the automotive industry, with iconic brands like **BMW, Audi**, and **Volkswagen**. Germany's picturesque landscapes, including **the Alps**, the **Black Forest**, and the **Rhine River**, attract nature lovers, while its vibrant cities, such as **Berlin, Munich**, and **Hamburg**, offer a mix of modernity

---

1   https://www.britannica.com/place/Germany

and historical charm. Additionally, Germany is globally recognized for its **beer culture**, epitomized by the famous **Oktoberfest**, and its unique traditions, such as **Christmas markets** and classical architecture.

Germany's history is marked by significant transformations and periods of division and unity. In the Middle Ages, the region was a collection of various kingdoms and principalities, united under the **Holy Roman Empire**. In 1871, the German Empire was formed under **Prussian leadership**, consolidating many German-speaking states. Following its defeat in World War I, the empire collapsed, giving way to the **Weimar Republic**, which struggled with economic instability and political unrest. The rise of Adolf Hitler and the **Nazi regime** led to World War II and the horrors of the Holocaust. After the war, Germany was divided into East and West, with **the West** becoming a **democratic republic** and **the East** a **socialist state** under Soviet influence. **The Berlin Wall**, symbolizing this division, fell in 1989, and Germany reunified in 1990. Since then, it has emerged as a stable democracy and global economic powerhouse.

The Capital

Berlin, the capital of Germany, is a dynamic city known for its rich history, cultural diversity, and modern vibrancy. Located in Northeastern Germany, Berlin has long been a **political** and **cultural center**, once the heart of the Kingdom of Prussia and later the capital of a unified Germany. The city endured significant destruction during World War II but was rebuilt and became the focal point of the Cold War, famously divided by **the Berlin Wall** from 1961 to 1989. Today, Berlin is **a global metropolis**, known for its eclectic mix of historic landmarks like the **Brandenburg Gate** and the **Berlin Wall Memorial**, as well as its thriving arts scene, trendy neighborhoods, and innovative architecture. It is also a **hub for politics, education, and business**, and continues to attract visitors from around the world with its unique blend of history, culture, and modernity.

The People

The people of Germany are known for their diversity, strong sense of community, and a deep commitment to order and efficiency. While the majority of the population is of German ethnic origin, the country has a long history of immigration, which has made it a **multicultural society**. Over the years, communities of Turkish, Italian, Polish, Greek, and other ethnic groups have settled in Germany, contributing to its rich cultural fabric. As a result, Germans today have a variety of backgrounds and heritage, with significant influence from both neighboring European countries and other regions. The people take pride in their history, but they also embrace modern values, including social welfare, environmentalism, and human rights.

Germans are often associated with qualities such as **punctuality, discipline**, and a **strong work ethic**. Family plays an important role in German society, and social life is often centered around gatherings, whether in family homes or local community events. Despite their reputation for being direct, Germans are also known for their **hospitality** and a **deep respect for privacy and personal space. Education** is highly valued, and Germany is home to some of **the world's best universities** and **research institutions**. The country's cultural life is equally rich, with Germans celebrating a variety of traditions, from Oktoberfest in Munich to Christmas markets in cities like Nuremberg and Cologne.

Language

The official language of Germany is **Standard German** (*Hochdeutsch*), which is widely spoken across the country. However, there are many regional dialects that vary by region, often influenced by neighboring countries such as France, Switzerland, and Austria. These dialects can sometimes be challenging to understand, even for native German speakers, but they reflect the country's rich linguistic diversity.

While German is the dominant language, many Germans are fluent in English, especially in urban areas and among younger generations, due to the country's international connections and strong educational system.

Religion

Christianity is the dominant religion in Germany, with **Roman Catholicism** and **Protestantism** (specifically Lutheranism) being the two most widely practiced branches. About 50 percent of the population identifies as Christian, with Catholics predominating in the southern and western parts of the country, while Protestants are more common in the north and east.

Christianity was introduced to the region during the early Middle Ages, and it remains deeply intertwined with the culture and traditions of the country. Over recent decades, **secularism** has grown, with an increasing number of Germans identifying as non-religious. There are also smaller communities of Muslims, Jews, Buddhists, and others, reflecting Germany's **multicultural society**.

Affordability

Germany can be considered a **relatively affordable destination** for travelers, though costs can vary depending on the region, type of accommodation, and activities. For budget-conscious travelers, Germany offers a range of options. **Public transportation**, such as trains, buses, and trams, is efficient and **reasonably priced**, especially with discounted passes or travel cards available for tourists. **Food** can also be **affordable**, particularly in local markets, street food stalls, and casual eateries. Traditional German meals like bratwurst, pretzels, and schnitzels can be found at lower prices compared to dining in more upscale restaurants or tourist-heavy areas.

Accommodation ranges from budget hostels and guesthouses to mid-range hotels, though prices tend to rise in major cities like Berlin, Munich, and Hamburg, particularly during peak tourist seasons. Rural areas and smaller towns can offer cheaper options. Many **cultural attractions**, such as museums, parks, and historical sites, are either **free** or have **low entrance fees**, making it easy to explore Germany without breaking the bank. However, popular events like Oktoberfest or major festivals may increase travel costs, with higher prices for accommodation and food. Overall, with proper planning and budgeting, Germany can be an affordable destination, especially for those who avoid peak tourist seasons and take advantage of budget-friendly options.

Germany, the Basics

How to Get There?

Germany is **well-connected** to the rest of the world, with numerous international airports offering direct flights from major cities around the globe. The country's transport infrastructure is excellent, and it's easy to travel to Germany by air, train, or even by road if you're already in Europe. Germany's biggest airports include:

- **Frankfurt Airport (FRA):** Located in the heart of Germany, Frankfurt is the busiest airport in the country and one of the largest in Europe. It serves as a major international hub for flights connecting Europe with Asia, North America, and other regions.

- **Munich Airport (MUC):** The second-largest airport in Germany, Munich's Franz Josef Strauss Airport serves as a key gateway to southern Germany and is a hub for flights within Europe and international routes, especially to Asia and North America.

- **Berlin Brandenburg Airport (BER):** The newest major airport in Germany, located just outside the city of Berlin. It replaced the older Tegel and Schönefeld airports, providing modern facilities for both domestic and international flights.

- **Düsseldorf Airport (DUS):** Serving the Rhine-Ruhr metropolitan region, Düsseldorf Airport is one of the busiest in Germany, with frequent flights to major European destinations as well as direct routes to Asia and North America.

- **Hamburg Airport (HAM):** Located in the northern part of Germany, Hamburg Airport is a key hub for flights to and from other European cities and various international destinations.

Germany's major airlines include **Lufthansa**, the country's flagship carrier and one of the largest in Europe, offering a broad range of domestic and international flights to destinations across Europe, North America,

Asia, and beyond. Based in Frankfurt and Munich, Lufthansa is known for its extensive network. **Eurowings**, a subsidiary of Lufthansa, provides low-cost flights primarily within Europe, though it also operates some long-haul international routes. Another key player is **Condor**, a German leisure airline offering flights to popular vacation destinations across Europe, Africa, and the Americas. While **Air Berlin** ceased operations in 2017, many of its former routes were absorbed by other airlines, including Lufthansa and **easyJet**, both of which are popular budget airlines offering affordable flights to Germany from a variety of European cities.

The best times to fly to Germany for **the cheapest rates** are typically during the **shoulder seasons**—in the early spring (March to May) and late fall (October to November). During these times, the weather is still pleasant, but the number of tourists is lower, resulting in cheaper flight tickets and accommodation prices.

The **off-season** months of winter (late November to February) can also offer cheaper flights, although the weather can be cold and some tourist attractions may be less accessible. However, if you're interested in experiencing Christmas markets or winter sports in places like the Bavarian Alps, this can still be a great time to visit.

Summer months (June to August) and **holiday periods like Christmas and New Year** tend to be the **most expensive** times to fly to Germany due to high demand from tourists. Booking flights well in advance during these peak seasons can help secure better prices.

Overall, for the cheapest flights, try to book at least three to six months in advance, and use flight comparison tools to monitor and find the best deals.

When to Visit?

Germany offers a variety of experiences depending on when you choose to visit, with each season bringing its own charm. Here's an overview of the best times to visit based on weather, crowd levels, and activities:

- **Weather-wise:** The best times to visit Germany are in **spring (April to June)** and **fall (September to October)**, offering mild temperatures and fewer tourists. **Summer (June to August)** is warm and popular, but can be crowded and expensive, while **winter (December to February)** is cold but ideal for winter sports and Christmas markets.

- **Crowd-wise: Peak season** is during the summer months, especially July and August, with high prices and large crowds. The **off-season** includes winter (November to February) and the **shoulder seasons** in spring and fall, offering fewer crowds and lower prices.

- **Best for Activities: Spring and summer** are great for outdoor activities like hiking and cycling, while **winter** is perfect for skiing and enjoying Christmas markets.

- **Festivals and Events:** Notable events include **Oktoberfest** (Munich, late September to early October), **Carnival** (February), **Christmas Markets** (November to December), and the **Berlinale** (Berlin, February).

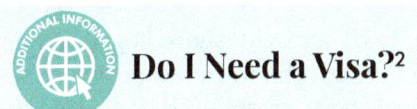 **Do I Need a Visa?**[2]

Whether you need a visa to visit Germany depends on your **nationality** and the purpose of your visit. Citizens of the **European Union (EU), European Economic Area (EEA)**, and **Switzerland do not require a visa** to enter Germany. Additionally, nationals from countries like the **United States, Canada, Australia**, and **Japan** can enter Germany **visa-free for stays of up to 90 days** within a 180-day period for tourism, business, or family visits, as part of the Schengen Area agreement. However, if you plan to stay for longer than 90 days or if your visit is for purposes such as work, study, or family reunification, you will need to apply for a **long-stay visa** or a **residence permit**. It's always advisable to check the latest visa requirements through the German embassy or consulate in your home country before making travel plans, as visa policies can change over time.

---

2   https://www.germany-visa.org/)

How to Get Around

Germany offers a variety of convenient transportation options for tourists, making it easy to get around whether you're visiting cities or exploring the countryside.

One of the most popular and efficient ways to travel within cities and between them is by **train**. The **Deutsche Bahn (DB)** operates an extensive and reliable rail network that connects major cities like Berlin, Munich, and Frankfurt, as well as smaller towns and rural areas. High-speed trains like the **ICE (InterCity Express)** make long-distance travel quick and comfortable. For regional travel, **regional trains** and **S-bahns (suburban trains)** are frequent and affordable.

In major cities, **public transportation** systems like buses, trams, and metro/subway lines are widely available. Cities such as Berlin, Munich, and Hamburg have well-organized public transit networks that are easy to navigate with day passes or multi-day travel cards offering unlimited rides.

For a more personalized experience, **taxis** and **rideshare services** like **Uber** are readily available, although they can be more expensive compared to public transport. If you're looking to travel on a budget, **bicycles** are a great option in many German cities, as they are bike-friendly with well-marked cycling lanes, and bike rentals are easy to find.

For more scenic or rural routes, **car rentals** are a good option, especially if you want to explore areas not easily accessible by public transportation. Germany's well-maintained highways (*Autobahnen*) make driving across the country smooth and straightforward, though it's important to note that some parts of the Autobahn have no speed limits.

Lastly, **flights** are an efficient way to travel between major cities if you're short on time, with Germany having several international airports that connect to the rest of Europe and the world. However, for short distances, taking the train is often a more convenient and scenic option.

Overall, Germany's public transportation system is highly reliable, efficient, and easy to use, making it a great choice for tourists wanting to explore the country.

Monetary Advice

The national currency of Germany is the **Euro** (€), and the exchange rate typically fluctuates against other currencies like the U.S. Dollar (USD), however at the time of writing of this book, the exchange rates is about **US$1 to €1.09**.

You can exchange foreign currency at banks, exchange bureaus, or ATMs throughout the country. It's recommended to check the exchange rate before converting large amounts of money to ensure you're getting a fair rate.

Credit cards are **widely accepted** in Germany, particularly in larger cities and tourist areas, with **Visa** and **Mastercard** being the most commonly accepted. However, smaller establishments, such as local restaurants or shops, may prefer **cash** or only accept **debit cards**. In such cases, it's always a good idea to have some **cash** on hand. **American Express** cards are less commonly accepted, so it's best to inquire beforehand if you plan to use one. When using credit cards, be mindful of potential **foreign transaction fees**, which some banks or card providers may charge. It's also recommended to inform your bank ahead of time about your travel plans to avoid any issues with card usage abroad.

While most businesses in Germany don't typically allow **bargaining** and prices are generally fixed in shops, restaurants, and service providers, you may find that negotiating prices is more common in markets, especially for souvenirs or certain goods. Still, this is less of a cultural norm compared to some other countries.

When it comes to **tipping**, it is customary but not obligatory. In restaurants, it's common to round up the bill or leave a tip of about **5-10 percent** of the total amount if the service was good. Tipping in cafes or for drinks is usually about €1-2 (about the same in USD). In taxis, rounding up the fare is also appreciated, and for hotel porters or concierge services, tipping €1-2 (about the same in USD) per bag is customary. While tipping is generally seen as a gesture of appreciation for good service, it's not as high-pressure as in some other countries, and the overall amount is often left to the discretion of the customer.

German Hospitality

There's a common misconception that Germans are cold, distant, and somewhat inhospitable. In reality, their hospitality is **rooted in formality** and **a deep respect for personal space.** While they may seem reserved at first, this is simply a cultural trait, and once you establish a connection, you'll find that Germans are warm and generous hosts. Their approach to hospitality is more about creating a comfortable, organized environment and showing respect for boundaries, rather than overt displays of warmth.

German hospitality is typically expressed through thoughtful gestures like inviting guests for a meal or drinks. It's common for Germans to serve hearty, traditional dishes such as sausages, schnitzels, or local pastries, often accompanied by beer, especially in regions like Bavaria. If you're invited to someone's home, it's polite to bring a small gift, such as wine, flowers, or chocolates, to show appreciation. They take pride in making their guests feel comfortable but also value efficiency, so things tend to be well-organized and on time.

When visiting Germany, there are several cultural norms you should be aware of. **Punctuality** is very important; being late is seen as disrespectful, so always try to arrive on time. **Formality in address** is also common. It's typical to use titles and last names until invited to switch to first names. **Personal space** is highly valued, so avoid standing too close to others in public or during conversation. Interrupting someone while they're speaking is considered rude, and Germans generally prefer **direct and honest communication**. It's also important to respect the local rules, whether it's about recycling, traffic, or social behavior. Finally, avoid discussing sensitive topics like politics or religion unless the conversation naturally leads to it, as these can be touchy subjects.

CUSTOMS

IN THIS CHAPTER

- Travelers Entering Germany
- Customs Entitlements and Monetary Restrictions
- Restricted and Prohibited Items
- Five Practical Tips to Know Before You Go

CHAPTER 2
CUSTOMS

Travelers Entering Germany[3]

To enter Germany, travelers typically need the following documents, but requirements may vary depending on nationality, travel purpose, and duration of stay:

- **Passport:** A valid passport is required for entry into Germany. For most non-EU travelers, it should be valid for at least three months beyond the planned departure date.

- **Visa:** Depending on your nationality and the purpose of your visit, you may need a visa. Citizens of many countries, including the U.S., Canada, and Australia, can enter Germany for short stays (up to 90 days) without a visa under the Schengen Area agreement. If you plan to stay longer or for purposes like work or study, you will need a specific visa.

- **Proof of Sufficient Funds:** You may need to show proof that you have enough financial resources for the duration of your stay, such as bank statements or a sponsor letter.

- **Travel Insurance:** Travel health insurance covering medical emergencies is highly recommended and may be required for long-term stays or specific types of visas.

---

3   https://www.axatravelinsurance.com/resources/guides/
     travel-requirements-germany

- **Return or Onward Travel Ticket:** You might be asked to provide proof of your return or onward travel from Germany.

When you land in Germany, you will go through standard customs and immigration procedures. You'll first proceed to **passport control**, where EU citizens use separate lanes from non-EU citizens. The immigration officer will check your passport, and if applicable, your visa. You may be asked about the purpose of your visit and the duration of your stay. After passport control, you will move on to customs. You may need to declare any restricted or controlled items like large sums of cash, certain goods, or food products. Since Germany is part of the **Schengen Area**, there are no routine border checks for travel within most European countries, but customs checks still apply for specific items. Depending on the airport, biometric screening, such as facial recognition or fingerprint scanning, may also be part of the process.

For the most reliable and up-to-date information, travelers should consult official websites such as the **German Federal Foreign Office**, which provides travel advisories and requirements. You can also check the **European Union's travel portal** for general travel guidelines or use the **IATA Travel Centre** to get information on flight restrictions and visa requirements. It's always a good idea to review these resources before your trip to ensure you have the latest details on entry requirements and any potential restrictions or changes.

Customs Entitlements and Monetary Restrictions

When entering Germany, there are specific customs entitlements and monetary restrictions to be aware of. These rules ensure that goods and currency are properly declared and that travelers comply with European Union (EU) regulations.

If you are traveling to Germany from a non-EU country, there are restrictions on the amount of currency or monetary instruments you can bring into the country without declaring it. Any traveler entering Germany with **€10,000** or more (approximately US$10,945) in cash, checks, or similar financial instruments must declare it to customs authorities.

Failure to declare amounts over this threshold can result in confiscation of the funds and possible fines. The same rule applies to travelers leaving Germany and other EU countries. If you're entering from another EU country, there's no limit on how much currency you can carry, but if you carry amounts over €10,000, you must be prepared to explain the source of the funds.

There are also guidelines on the types and quantities of goods that can be brought into Germany, especially when traveling from non-EU countries. Here are the key points to keep in mind:

- **Alcohol:** You can bring in **up to 1 liter** (33.8 oz) of spirits with an alcohol content over 22 percent, or **2 liters** (67.6 oz) of alcohol with an alcohol content of 22 percent or less (like wine or champagne), without paying customs duties. Additionally, up to **4 liters** (135.3 oz) of non-alcoholic beverages are allowed.

- **Tobacco:** You are allowed to bring in up to 800 cigarettes, 400 cigarillos, 200 cigars, or 1 kg of tobacco without paying customs duties. The amount must be for personal use only and not intended for resale.

- **Food and Plants:** There are restrictions on bringing in certain food items, especially meat and dairy products, as well as plants and plant-based products due to concerns about diseases or pests. For example, bringing meat from non-EU countries is generally prohibited. If you are traveling from another EU country, you can bring most food items without restrictions, but some products like raw milk or unprocessed meat may still have limitations.

- **Personal Goods:** Personal goods like clothing, electronics, and other personal items are typically allowed without issue, as long as they are for personal use and not intended for resale. However, if you're carrying large quantities of items or goods that seem to be for commercial purposes, you may be required to declare them and pay customs duties.

- **Medicines:** If you need to bring prescription medicines into Germany, you should carry them in their original packaging, along with a doctor's prescription or a letter explaining the medical need. Some controlled substances may require special permits.

In addition to these guidelines, travelers should be aware that customs authorities can request **proof of purchase for items**, so it's helpful to keep receipts for expensive or high-value goods. If you exceed the duty-free limits for any category, you may need to pay customs duties or taxes, and failure to declare goods when required can result in fines or the seizure of the goods.

For more specific information about customs entitlements and restrictions, you can refer to the **German Customs website** or consult the **European Union's customs rules**, which apply across all EU member states. It's always a good idea to check the latest regulations before your trip, as customs rules can change.

 ## Restricted and Prohibited Items[4]

When traveling to Germany, certain items are either prohibited or restricted. These items may not only violate the country's laws but can also pose security risks, health concerns, or impact public safety. Here's an overview of the categories and specific items that are restricted or prohibited:

- **Narcotics and Controlled Substances:** Illegal drugs, including marijuana, heroin, and other substances classified as controlled under German law.

- **Weapons and Ammunition:** Firearms, explosives, and other weapons without proper authorization. This includes stun guns, pepper spray (unless for personal self-defense), and certain knives.

- **Fake or Counterfeit Items:** Fake goods, including counterfeit currency, fake designer clothing or accessories.

- **Pornographic Materials:** Materials considered to violate German laws on decency or that involve minors or non-consensual content.

---

4   https://www.hinterlandtravel.com/germany/customs

- **Extremist Propaganda:** Any form of media or material promoting hatred, violence, or terrorism, such as Nazi symbols, hate speech materials, or materials promoting extremist ideologies.

- **Endangered Species and Products Made from Them:** Items made from or containing parts of endangered species, including ivory, furs, and exotic plants or animals.

Bringing prohibited items into Germany can lead to **confiscation**, **fines**, and **criminal prosecution**. Serious offenses, such as possessing illegal drugs, weapons, or extremist materials, can result in **arrest** and **imprisonment**. In extreme cases, you may be **deported** and **banned** from re-entering the country. Legal action may also be taken, particularly for high-value counterfeit goods. For the most accurate and up-to-date information on prohibited items when entering Germany, consult the official website of the **German Customs Authority (Zoll)**.

 ## Five Practical Tips to Know Before You Go

Germany is a country with rich traditions and cultural norms that can be quite different from what travelers might be used to. To make the most of your trip and avoid any awkward moments, it's helpful to familiarize yourself with a few key customs. Here are five practical tips to keep in mind before you go, ensuring that you respect German culture and have a smooth, enjoyable visit:

1. **Be Punctual:** Punctuality is highly valued in Germany. Whether for business or social events, always arrive on time, as being late is considered disrespectful.

2. **Respect Personal Space:** Germans value personal space. Maintain distance in lines and during conversations and use a formal handshake when greeting people.

3. **Observe "Quiet Hours":** Germany has designated "quiet hours" from 10:00 PM to 6:00 AM, especially in residential areas. Avoid loud noises during these times to respect neighbors.

4. **Follow Recycling Practices:** Recycling is important in Germany. Separate your trash into designated bins for paper, plastic, glass, and organic waste.

5. **Don't Tip Excessively:** While tipping is appreciated, it's not obligatory or even expected as in some other countries. In restaurants, rounding up the bill or leaving a 5-10 percent tip is sufficient.

CHAPTER 3

CRIME IN GERMANY

CRIME IN GERMANY

Overview[5]

Germany is generally considered to be a **safe country**, with a **relatively low crime rate** compared to many other nations, especially within Europe. The country is known for its well-developed infrastructure, strong rule of law, and efficient law enforcement, which contribute to the overall safety of both residents and visitors.

Several factors contribute to crime in Germany, including **economic disparities**, **social issues**, **immigration**, and **organized crime**. While Germany has a strong economy, like many countries, economic inequality can sometimes lead to property crimes or drug-related offenses. The country also faces challenges related to **immigration**, which has led to some debates around crime and integration. However, there is no clear correlation between immigration and rising crime, as statistics show that immigrants are less likely to commit violent crimes than native-born citizens. Additionally, **organized crime**—especially involving drug trafficking, human trafficking, and illegal arms trade—continues to be a concern, particularly in major cities.

Over recent years, **crime rates in Germany have generally been stable or decreasing**, especially when it comes to violent crime. According to

---

5   https://www.bka.de/EN/CurrentInformation/Statistics/
     PoliceCrimeStatistics/policecrimestatistics_node.html

the German Federal Criminal Police Office (BKA), the overall crime rate saw a decrease in the last decade. **Property crimes**, including burglary, car theft, and pickpocketing, have been on a **downward trend**, while **cybercrime** and **online fraud** have risen, reflecting global digital security challenges. In particular, **violent crime** has remained low, and **homicides** are rare in Germany compared to other countries. However, there has been a notable **increase in crimes related to drugs** and **domestic violence** in recent years.

Overall, while Germany remains one of the safest countries in Europe, the trends show a shift toward non-violent crimes, particularly those related to technology.

Crime Hotspots in Germany

In Germany, certain areas have **higher crime rates**, particularly **larger cities** and **urban regions. Berlin,** as the capital, sees a significant amount of property crime, including pickpocketing, burglary, and vehicle theft, especially in tourist-heavy areas. **Frankfurt**, known for its financial district, faces challenges related to organized crime, drug trafficking, and violence, particularly around its central train station. **Hamburg**, as a major port city, experiences issues with drug-related crime and organized crime, particularly in the Reeperbahn area, which is known for street violence, prostitution, and drug trafficking. **Düsseldorf** and **Cologne** also have higher crime rates in certain parts of the city, with pickpocketing and scams being more common in crowded, tourist-oriented locations like shopping districts and major landmarks. While these cities experience higher crime rates compared to rural areas, **Germany remains a safe country overall.**

For the latest crime information, travelers can refer to official travel advisory websites, such as the **U.S. Department of State's travel advisory for Germany** or the **UK's Foreign Travel Advice**, both of which provide updated information about safety risks and crime trends.

In terms of international comparisons, Germany's crime rates, especially for violent crimes like homicide and armed robbery, are much lower than those in the United States. For example, Germany's homicide rate is around 0.9 per 100,000 people, while the U.S. has a significantly higher rate of 6.9 per 100,000 people. Although Germany has seen an increase in cybercrime and drug-related offenses, its overall violent crime rates are far lower than those in the U.S., making it a safer destination for travelers.[6]

Crime Statistics

In Germany, violent crimes and non-violent crimes differ significantly in both their frequency and nature. **Violent crimes**, which involve physical harm or the threat of harm to individuals, are relatively rare compared to global averages. These include offenses such as homicide, assault, robbery, and sexual violence, with the homicide rate being approximately 0.8 per 100,000 people. While violent crime does occur, it is typically concentrated in **specific urban areas** or **associated with gang violence or domestic disputes**.

In contrast, **non-violent crimes**, which primarily involve property damage or financial harm, are **more common** in Germany. Theft, burglary, pickpocketing, and car break-ins are frequent, especially in tourist-heavy regions. Non-violent crimes also encompass growing issues like fraud, cybercrime, and online scams, which have become increasingly prevalent with the rise of digital platforms.

For tourists, the most common crimes they face in Germany are **theft**, particularly **pickpocketing** in major cities, and **scams**. Common scams include overcharging for services like taxis or restaurants and individuals pretending to be legitimate charity collectors. While violent crimes like **street robberies** and **assaults** are not frequent, tourists should still remain cautious, especially when traveling at night or in poorly lit areas. **Sexual harassment** or assault can occur, particularly in crowded festivals like Oktoberfest or on public transportation during peak times, though Germany has strict laws protecting victims, and incidents are usually reported quickly.

---

6   https://bjs.ojp.gov/content/pub/pdf/gap.pdf

Another concern for tourists is **car break-ins**, especially those who rent vehicles and leave valuables inside, as well as **cycling accidents**, as Germany's extensive cycling infrastructure sometimes leads to accidents, particularly for those unfamiliar with the roads.

 ## Quick Safety Tips

- Keep track of local news and be aware of any spikes in crime, particularly those targeting tourists. Staying updated can help you avoid risky situations.

- For immediate emergencies, dial **112**. Familiarize yourself with local emergency services and procedures to respond quickly if needed.

- Show respect to the people and their traditions. Adhering to cultural norms will help you avoid misunderstandings or conflicts.

- Always use well-lit, busy stations, and avoid lingering alone for too long. Knowing the transportation options and their operating hours will help you stay safe.

- While civil unrest is rare in Germany, it can still occur. Stay informed and avoid areas where protests or political demonstrations are happening to stay clear of potential disturbances.

CHAPTER 4

CRIMINAL LAW VIOLATIONS

CHAPTER 4

CRIMINAL LAW VIOLATIONS

Marijuana and Other Drugs in Germany[7]

Germany's relationship with cannabis has evolved over time. For most of the 20th century, cannabis was viewed with suspicion, particularly after World War II, with drug control policies being strongly influenced by international norms and concerns about addiction. Cannabis was classified as a dangerous substance, and its use was criminalized.

In the 1970s, as drug use became more widespread globally, discussions on cannabis in Germany began to shift. This was partly due to the growing recognition that cannabis, unlike other substances, did not carry the same level of health risks or addictive properties. Despite these developments, cannabis remained illegal for both recreational and medical use.

Recently, Germany has taken significant steps in the medical use of cannabis. **In 2017, the country legalized medical cannabis use for patients suffering from severe health conditions** like chronic pain, multiple sclerosis, and chemotherapy-induced nausea. Medical cannabis is available in various forms, including dried flowers, oils, and capsules. Patients **must receive a prescription from a licensed physician**, and the prescription can only be provided when other treatments have failed. **Health insurance in Germany typically covers the cost of medical**

---

7   https://en.wikipedia.org/wiki/Cannabis_in_Germany

cannabis for patients who meet specific criteria, although not all insurance companies provide coverage for this treatment.

The **Cannabis Act**, effective **April 1, 2024, legalized recreational use for adults under certain restrictions**; it is legal for adults in Germany to possess **25 grams (7/8 oz) or less of cannabis in public**, up to **50 grams (1¾ oz) of dried cannabis in private**, and have up to **three flowering cannabis plants** at home for personal use.

Synthetic cannabinoids, designed to mimic THC, are illegal due to their greater potency and unpredictable health consequences, and are classified as controlled substances under **the German Narcotics Act**. These cannabinoids have been **a concern in Germany** due to their prevalence in the black market, particularly in "legal highs" sold in head shops or online. However, due to the constant evolution of new synthetic cannabinoid formulations, enforcement and regulation remain challenging.[8]

Germany has a well-established framework for dealing with other controlled substances, including **illegal drugs** such as heroin, cocaine, methamphetamines, and ecstasy. Possessing illegal drugs in Germany is a **criminal offense**. However, the country has adopted more harm reduction strategies in recent years, including needle exchange programs and supervised injection rooms, particularly for heroin users in cities like Berlin and Frankfurt.[9]

Trafficking and **dealing** in illegal drugs are severely punished in Germany, with sentences ranging from several years to life imprisonment, depending on the severity of the offense. There have been ongoing discussions about decriminalizing certain substances, especially for personal use, but there is still no consensus on moving away from criminal penalties for possession of drugs like heroin, cocaine, and ecstasy.

---

8   https://en.wikipedia.org/wiki/Synthetic_cannabinoids

9   https://www.drugpolicyfacts.org/node/4048

Penalties[10]

Germany's drug laws are stringent, with distinct penalties for the possession, distribution, and cultivation of marijuana, as well as for other illegal substances. While cannabis has been **partially legalized** since **April 2024**, personal use within certain limits is permitted, but exceeding these limits can lead to significant legal consequences.

Under the **Cannabis Act**, adults are allowed to possess **up to 25 grams** of cannabis in public and store **up to 50 grams** at home. Cultivating **up to three plants** for personal use is also legal. However, exceeding these amounts can result in **fines or imprisonment**, particularly if there is evidence of intent to distribute. For relatively minor offenses exceeding the limits, administrative penalties may be imposed instead of jail time.

Public consumption is tightly regulated, with fines of up to **€30,000** (about US\$33,170) for violations. **Public consumption** is also **restricted between 7 a.m. and 8 p.m.** in pedestrian zones to protect children and maintain public order.

While personal use is now legal within set limits, the **distribution and sale** of cannabis remain **criminal offenses** unless conducted through authorized channels like licensed cannabis clubs. The **unauthorized sale of cannabis** can lead to prison sentences of **up to three years**, with penalties escalating for larger quantities or aggravating factors such as trafficking to minors or organized crime involvement. Selling or sharing cannabis outside legal frameworks is prohibited, with penalties reaching up to **five years** in prison in severe cases.

Cultivation of more than three cannabis plants for personal use is also illegal and can result in **up to three years in prison**. Homegrown cannabis must not be shared with others, and cultivation must not cause unreasonable disturbance to neighbors. New rules that allow cultivation through **non-profit cannabis clubs** will enable individuals to grow

---

10   https://kummuni.com/cannabis-in-germany/, https://www.drugpolicy-facts.org/region/germany

cannabis collectively, provided they comply with strict regulations, including age restrictions and membership limits.

The legal approach to **synthetic cannabinoids** differs from that of natural cannabis. Synthetic cannabinoids are treated more harshly due to their health risks and are subject to penalties of **up to three years in prison**, or **up to ten years for more serious offenses** such as trafficking. This stricter stance reflects the increased danger these substances pose compared to natural marijuana.

For other drugs, such as **heroin, cocaine,** or **methamphetamines**, penalties are similarly severe. Possessing small quantities for personal use can lead to fines or alternative measures like treatment or community service, depending on the drug and the circumstances. **Larger amounts** or drugs intended for distribution can result in **up to five years in prison.** Some states have set specific thresholds for what constitutes a "small amount" of certain drugs, such as one gram of cocaine in Hamburg or 0.5 grams in North Rhine-Westphalia.

The law provides alternatives to criminal punishment for those caught with small quantities, including **drug counseling** and **rehabilitation programs.** For **first-time offenses** involving certain drugs, prosecution may not always occur, and individuals may receive treatment instead of jail time.

Importantly, drug convictions can affect an individual's **immigration status.** A sentence of more than **90 days** may prevent individuals from applying for citizenship or renewing their residence permits. Additionally, **driving under the influence** of cannabis or other drugs is illegal, with penalties including **fines, driving bans,** and **license suspensions.** The government has proposed new regulations for THC levels in drivers' blood, further tightening control over impaired driving.

As cannabis reforms continue to evolve, the future of the **Cannabis Act** remains uncertain. Shifts in political leadership, particularly the rise of conservative parties, could lead to the rollback of recent changes. While current cannabis laws reflect a shift toward personal freedom, they remain subject to ongoing political debates and may change as the legal and social landscape evolves.

Prescription Medication

You can travel to Germany with prescription medication, but there are specific regulations you need to follow. You are allowed to bring medications for your personal use, usually **up to a three-month supply**. Medications should remain in their **original packaging, clearly labeled** with your name, the prescribing doctor's information, and dosage instructions. It is strongly advised to carry a **copy of your prescription and a letter from your doctor** that explains your need for the medication, also supported by CDC guidelines.

If your medication is classified as a narcotic or controlled substance (for example, certain painkillers, ADHD medication, or anti-anxiety drugs), you will need to meet additional requirements. You must obtain a **Schengen certificate** under Article 75 of the Schengen Implementing Convention. This form must be completed by your doctor and certified by the appropriate health authority before your trip. The Schengen certificate is valid for **up to 30 days** and is required even if the drug is legally prescribed in your home country.

Upon entering Germany, if you are carrying a controlled substance or a large quantity of any medication, you **must declare** it at customs. German customs officials may ask to inspect your medications and verify their legitimacy.[11] It is best practice to carry your medications in your carry-on luggage so that they are accessible during your flight. If possible, you should also have your prescription and doctor's note translated into German to facilitate communication with customs or law enforcement if needed. Additionally, some medications that are available over-the-counter in other countries might be classified as controlled substances

---

11   https://www.zoll.de/EN/Private-individuals/Travel/Entering-Germany/ Restrictions/Medicinal-products-and-narcotics/medicinal-prod- ucts-and-narcotics_node.html

in Germany, so it is important to check the specific legal status of each medication before traveling.

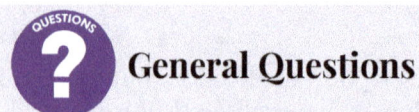

General Questions

1. *Is cannabis legal in Germany?* **Yes**. Cannabis is legal in Germany. However, possession of marijuana is accompanied by strict restrictions.

2. *Where can I legally purchase marijuana in Germany?* The only places to legally purchase marijuana in Germany are from licensed dispensaries found across the country, or from a legally licensed online provider, usually an online dispensary with delivery options.

3. *Can I have marijuana on my person or in a hotel room in Germany?* **Yes**. It is legal to have marijuana on your person or in a hotel room in Germany. However, it cannot be smoked indoors and can only be used in designated smoking areas.

4. *Are there any exceptions to the possession and consumption of cannabis in Germany?* **Yes**. There are exceptions to the possession and consumption of cannabis in Germany. Public consumption is prohibited in areas near schools, playgrounds, and in pedestrian zones during certain hours. Possession is limited to **25 grams in public** and **50 grams at home**, with any excess leading to fines or imprisonment. Cultivating more than three cannabis plants for personal use is illegal. Cannabis consumption is also banned in specific public spaces, and synthetic cannabinoids are subject to harsher penalties due to their higher health risks.

5. ***What are the penalties for possessing and consuming other types of illicit drugs in Germany?*** In Germany, penalties for possessing and consuming illicit drugs other than cannabis are severe. For small amounts intended for personal use, offenders may face fines, drug counseling, or community service. However, for larger quantities or distribution, penalties can include up to five years in prison. The law differentiates between small and larger amounts, with thresholds varying by state. First-time offenders with small quantities may sometimes avoid prosecution if they enter treatment programs.

 ## Law of the Land Hypothetical

HYPOTHETICAL: *John, a 32-year-old tourist from the United States, visits Berlin for a vacation. While strolling through a busy public square, he is stopped by the police for a routine check. During the search, the police find that John is carrying 30 grams of cannabis in his backpack. John explains that he bought the cannabis for personal use during his trip and was unaware of the legal limits for possession in Germany. He does not have any intention to sell or distribute the cannabis. As a tourist, what legal penalties could John face for possessing 30 grams of cannabis in a public place?*

ANSWER: *John has exceeded the 25-gram limit for public possession by 5 grams. As a tourist, he is still subject to German law. Since the amount is small and there's no intent to distribute, John is unlikely to face imprisonment. He will probably receive a fine or administrative penalty for exceeding the limit. Authorities may detain him briefly but are unlikely to press criminal charges unless there's evidence of trafficking or a significantly larger amount.*

Takeaways

- Cannabis is legal for personal use in Germany with restrictions. Adults can possess up to **25 grams in public, 50 grams at home**, and grow up to **three plants for personal use.** Exceeding these limits can lead to fines or imprisonment.

- Public consumption is banned in certain areas, especially near schools, playgrounds, and in pedestrian zones during specific hours. Violations can result in heavy fines (up to €30,000, or approximately US$34,180).

- Synthetic cannabinoids are illegal in Germany due to their higher health risks, with penalties of up to **three years in prison**, or up to **ten years** for more serious offenses like trafficking.

- Possession of other illicit drugs, such as heroin, cocaine, and methamphetamines, is also heavily penalized. Small amounts may lead to fines or treatment programs, while larger quantities or distribution can result in up to **five years in prison.**

- Drug convictions can affect immigration status in Germany. A sentence of more than 90 days can prevent individuals from applying for citizenship or renewing their residence permits.

CHAPTER 5

ALCOHOL-RELATED OFFENSES

IN THIS CHAPTER

- Alcohol-Related Offenses
- Alcohol Regulation
- Things to Remember
- General Questions
- Law of the Land Hypothetical
- Takeaways

CHAPTER 5

ALCOHOL-RELATED OFFENSES

Alcohol-Related Offenses

Alcohol plays a significant role in German culture and everyday life. Historically, Germany has a long tradition of brewing and consuming alcohol, particularly beer, which is deeply embedded in the country's social and cultural fabric. The **German Beer Purity Law** (*Reinheitsgebot*) **of 1516**, which regulated the ingredients allowed in beer, highlights the importance of alcohol in the nation's history. Over the years, beer became a symbol of national pride and an essential part of social gatherings.

Alcohol is widely consumed in Germany, with **beer** being the most popular alcoholic beverage. It is common to see people enjoying beer at family gatherings, outdoor events, and traditional beer gardens. Additionally, Germany is known for its **wine culture**, particularly in regions like the Mosel and Rhineland, where local wines, such as Riesling, are celebrated. **Schnapps** and other spirits are also consumed, often after meals or during social occasions. Germany remains one of the highest consumers of alcohol in Europe, with each person consuming approximately 91.6 liters of beer, 20.7 liters of wine, 3.2 liters of sparkling wine, and 5.2 liters of spirits per year.[12]

---

12 https://movendi.ngo/policy-updates/germany-alcohol-use-declines-as-affordability-falls-and-more-youth-stay-alcohol-free-longer/

Alcohol is **legal and widely available** in Germany. It is sold in supermarkets, convenience stores, and specialty shops, with a variety of beverages catering to different tastes. The **legal drinking age for beer and wine is 16**, while **spirits** are restricted to those **18 and older**. Public consumption of alcohol is generally accepted, and drinking in public places such as parks, streets, and festivals is common. Alcohol consumption is also part of many traditional events, including Oktoberfest in Munich, which celebrates beer culture.

Although alcohol is legally available, there are **regulations and restrictions**. Drunk driving laws are strict, with a **blood alcohol concentration (BAC) limit of 0.05 percent** for general drivers, and **0.0 percent for novice and commercial drivers**.[13] Violations of these laws can result in heavy fines, license suspensions, or even imprisonment. Public intoxication is generally tolerated, but disruptive behavior or dangerous conduct can lead to fines or arrest.

Alcohol Regulation[14]

In Germany, alcohol consumption is regulated by the **German Alcohol Act** (*Gesetz über die Kontrolle von Branntwein und alkoholischen Getränken*), which governs the production, sale, and consumption of alcoholic beverages. While alcohol is widely available, there are specific regulations in place to ensure public safety and health, particularly concerning public intoxication, drunk driving, and underage drinking.

There are also strict **restrictions on alcohol advertising** in Germany. Ads must not target minors or promote irresponsible drinking behavior. Advertising campaigns cannot suggest that drinking alcohol enhances personal success, attractiveness, or social status. Additionally, alcohol advertisements on television and radio are often restricted to certain times, avoiding programming aimed at younger audiences. Sponsorships

---

13 https://etsc.eu/issues/drink-driving/
    blood-alcohol-content-bac-drink-driving-limits-across-europe/

14 https://lawforeverything.com/alcohol-laws-in-germany/

by alcohol brands are also limited, especially in contexts where minors may be present, such as sports events.

Alcohol regulations are enforced by local authorities, police, and traffic enforcement officers. Violations of alcohol laws can lead to significant penalties. For example, Germany has a **0.05 percent blood alcohol concentration (BAC) limit for general drivers** and **0.00 percent BAC for novice drivers**. Anyone found exceeding these limits can face **fines**, **license suspension**, and possibly **imprisonment**, depending on the severity of the offense. While public drinking is generally tolerated, public intoxication that leads to **disruptive behavior** can result in **fines or detention**. Furthermore, selling alcohol to minors or allowing them to consume alcohol in public spaces can lead to fines or legal action against those responsible, including parents or vendors.

As mentioned above, Germany follows a **two-tiered legal drinking age** system. For **beer and wine**, the legal drinking age is **16 years old**, allowing minors aged 16 and above to consume these beverages in public. However, individuals **under 18** are **prohibited from purchasing or consuming spirits and stronger alcoholic drinks** such as schnapps or vodka. Police officers are tasked with ensuring that these regulations are followed in public spaces and businesses.

 **Things to Remember**

- **Drinking Age:** 18
- **ID:** An ID is required to purchase alcohol, especially if the one purchasing the alcohol doesn't look the legal age.
- **Public consumption:** It is legal to drink on the streets and carry around open containers.
- **Public drunkenness:** If the public drunkenness leads to disruptive or destructive behavior, the authorities have the right to arrest the individual.
- **Drunk Driving:** Drunk driving is illegal and strictly enforced.

- **Purchase of alcohol:** Alcohol can be purchased anywhere in Germany; the only stipulation is that certain types are sold in specific places.

- **Alcohol Permits:** if you intend to serve or sell alcohol at a party or event, you generally need a permit, especially if it's a commercial or public event, or if you are operating a business serving alcohol on a permanent basis.

 **General Questions**

1. *Can I drink and drive in Germany?* **No.** Drinking and driving is strictly prohibited in Germany, and the law is heavily enforced. Offenders can face immediate fines, suspension of their driver's license, and, in more severe cases, imprisonment, especially if their blood alcohol concentration (BAC) exceeds the legal limit. Penalties vary depending on the severity of the offense.

2. *Can I possess an open container in public?* **Yes.** In Germany, it is generally legal to possess and consume alcohol in public spaces, including parks, streets, and public transportation, as long as you are not being disruptive, destructive, or causing a public disturbance. However, local municipalities may have specific regulations or restrictions, particularly in certain public areas or during certain hours, like around schools or playgrounds. Public intoxication that leads to disorderly behavior can result in fines or even arrest.

Law of the Land Hypothetical

HYPOTHETICAL: *Sarah, a 24-year-old tourist from the United States, is visiting Munich during Oktoberfest. While walking through a public park, she opens a bottle of beer and enjoys a few drinks throughout the afternoon. As evening approaches, she becomes slightly intoxicated. A police officer approaches, notices she is drunk, but Sarah is not causing any trouble. Can Sarah be penalized for drinking alcohol in a public park in Munich, even though she wasn't causing a disturbance?*

ANSWER: *In general, public drinking is allowed in Germany, including in parks, as long as there is no disruption. However, some municipalities may have restrictions, especially during events like Oktoberfest. Since Sarah wasn't causing any issues, she is unlikely to face a penalty for drinking in the park. However, if local laws or event-specific rules prohibit drinking in certain areas, she could face fines. As long as her behavior remains non-disruptive, Sarah is likely in the clear, but it's always important to be aware of local regulations.*

Takeaways

- Alcohol, particularly beer, is integral to German culture, with a rich history in brewing. Beer is central to social events and festivals like Oktoberfest, and Germany's Beer Purity Law (*Reinheitsgebot*) of 1516 emphasizes its cultural significance.

- The legal drinking age is **16 for beer and wine**, and **18 for spirits**. Strict laws prevent underage drinking, with penalties for both underage drinkers and those providing alcohol to minors.

- Public drinking is allowed in most places, but disruptive behavior due to alcohol consumption can lead to fines or arrest. Local laws may impose additional restrictions, particularly near schools or playgrounds.

- Germany enforces strict drunk driving laws, with a BAC limit of 0.05 percent for regular drivers and 0.00 percent for novice and commercial drivers. Violating these limits can lead to fines, license suspension, or imprisonment.

- Alcohol advertising is regulated to prevent targeting minors or promoting irresponsible drinking. Ads are restricted to certain times, and alcohol brand sponsorships are limited in youth-related settings.

FIREARM & AMMUNITION OFFENSES

CHAPTER 6

FIREARM & AMMUNITION OFFENSES

Current Firearm Status[15]

In Germany, firearm ownership is tightly regulated. Only individuals who meet strict legal criteria and undergo thorough background checks are legally allowed to own a firearm. These individuals must be **over 18 years of age**, have no criminal record, and pass mental and physical fitness tests to demonstrate they are capable of safely handling a weapon. Additionally, prospective gun owners must prove a valid need for the firearm, such as for hunting or sport shooting.

The types of firearms legally allowed in Germany are limited. Civilians are permitted to own certain **handguns** and **semi-automatic firearms**, but military-grade weapons such as fully automatic or semi-automatic rifles, machine guns, and pump-action shotguns are banned. Antique firearms (pre-WWII) may be allowed under specific conditions.

To possess a firearm legally, individuals must obtain a **Weapons Possession Card** (*Waffenbesitzkarte*) for ownership and a **Weapons License** (*Waffenschein*) for carrying or using the weapon in public. While firearms like handguns and rifles can be owned, there are possession limits. For example, firearms must be kept securely and are subject

---

15 https://www.gunfinder.com/articles/75967

to regular inspections. Carrying a firearm in public is not generally permitted unless for specific purposes, such as hunting in designated areas.

The use of firearms in Germany is strictly regulated. **The only lawful purposes for using a firearm are those related to hunting or sport shooting in designated areas.** Even in these cases, the individual must have the necessary permits, including a *Waffenschein* and *Waffenbesitzkarte*. **Self-defense with a firearm is allowed only under very specific conditions and is subject to strict scrutiny.** Any use of a firearm outside these contexts is illegal and can result in severe penalties, including imprisonment.

Firearm Restrictions for Visitors

Non-citizens and visitors to Germany are subject to strict firearm regulations, and they are **generally not allowed to bring firearms into the country for personal use.** The only exception is for individuals who are legally permitted to import firearms under special circumstances, such as those coming for hunting or sporting events. However, this requires **prior approval from German authorities** and must be done through licensed companies or individuals with proper authorization.

Tourists wishing to bring their own firearms, such as U.S. citizens with personal guns, are not permitted to do so under normal circumstances. All firearms brought into Germany must be **declared in advance** and meet the requirements of German customs law. Even in cases where the firearm is imported legally, it must be stored and transported in accordance with strict regulations, including being unloaded and locked in a secure container.[16] For any non-citizen wishing to engage in activities that require a firearm, such as hunting or shooting sports, they must first obtain the appropriate permits and meet the same stringent requirements as German citizens. These include passing medical and mental health evaluations and demonstrating a valid reason for needing a

---

16   https://www.zoll.de/EN/Private-individuals/Travel/Travel-within-the-EU/Restrictions/Weapons-and-ammunition/weapons-and-ammunition_node.html

firearm, such as participation in a recognized sporting event or hunting trip.

 **Penalties**

Germany has strict penalties for offenses related to firearms, with harsh consequences for violations. Below are key penalties for various firearm-related offenses:

- **Possession of Illegal Firearms:** Individuals found in possession of illegal firearms may face up to **five years** in prison or a **fine**. The penalty can be more severe if the weapon is deemed particularly dangerous or if the individual has prior convictions.

- **Trafficking and Smuggling Firearms:** Those caught trafficking firearms, including smuggling them into the country, can face up to **10 years in prison**. The penalties are especially severe if the firearms are trafficked for criminal organizations or if they are intended for illegal use.

- **Firearm Use in Crimes:** Using a firearm in the commission of a crime (e.g., robbery, assault, or murder) significantly increases the severity of the penalty. For example, using a firearm during a robbery can result in an additional **five years** to the prison sentence for the underlying crime. If the firearm is used in a homicide, the individual may face **life imprisonment**. Additionally, if a firearm is used in the commission of a violent crime or if it results in injury or death, the penalties can be severe and include long-term imprisonment.

- **Unauthorized Carrying of Firearms:** Carrying a firearm without the necessary permits or in violation of firearm transport regulations can lead to a **prison sentence of up to three years** or a **fine**. If the firearm is carried without the appropriate legal justification, such as for hunting or sporting purposes, the penalty can be particularly harsh.

- **Penalties for Organized Crime Involvement:** Involvement in organized crime with firearms carries some of the harshest penalties. If an individual is caught trafficking firearms as part of a criminal organization or using firearms in organized crime activities, they can face **up to 10 years in prison**, or in some cases, **life imprisonment** if the crimes are particularly violent or result in death.

 ## General Questions

1. *What happens if the police catch me carrying a firearm in Germany?* If you are caught with a firearm in Germany, law enforcement will likely ask for the necessary permits to legally own a weapon in the country. If you cannot provide these permits, you will be immediately arrested, and the firearm will be confiscated. Additionally, if it is determined that you were carrying the weapon without proper authorization, you could face significant fines and a prison sentence.

2. *What is the potential sentence for a firearms violation upon conviction?* The potential sentence for a firearms violation upon conviction can include a minimum of five years imprisonment, along with a significant fine. Additionally, the person's firearm permits and any legally owned firearms will be confiscated.

Law of the Land True Story

In a significant ruling on July 1, 2024, the Düsseldorf Administrative Court determined that members of the far-right Alternative for Germany (AfD) party cannot legally possess firearms under Germany's weapons law. This decision stems from the classification of the AfD as a suspected extremist group by the country's domestic intelligence agency, the BfV, which has accused the party of attempting to undermine Germany's democratic constitution.

The court's ruling involved a married couple who had been ordered to surrender their firearms after their possession permits were revoked. The husband owned 197 firearms, while the wife had 27. They were also required to relinquish any ammunition. This legal precedent underscores Germany's strict approach to firearm ownership, particularly in cases involving individuals linked to extremist political movements. The decision also has broader implications for other AfD members, as the court allowed for an appeal. If upheld, the ruling could limit firearm ownership among individuals associated with groups deemed to be a threat to Germany's democratic institutions.

Takeaways

- Only individuals who are over 18, pass mental and physical fitness tests, have no criminal record, and demonstrate a valid need (e.g., hunting or sport shooting) can own a firearm. Military-grade weapons are prohibited for civilians.

- Possessing illegal firearms can result in up to five years in prison, trafficking firearms can lead to up to 10 years, and using a firearm in a crime adds significant prison time. Unauthorized carrying can result in up to three years or a fine.

- Firearms can only be used for hunting or sport shooting in designated areas. Self-defense with firearms is allowed only under strict conditions. Unauthorized use is illegal and penalized.

- Non-citizens are generally prohibited from bringing firearms into Germany. Special permits are required for hunting or sport shooting, and strict regulations govern firearm storage and transportation.

- Even legal gun owners in Germany must adhere to strict storage and transport regulations. Firearms must be securely stored and transported in a locked, unloaded condition, with the safety engaged. Carrying a firearm in public is only allowed under specific conditions.

CHAPTER 7

PROSTITUTION

IN THIS CHAPTER

- Overview
- Laws and Penalties
- Prostitution Practices
- Sex Trafficking and Exploitation
- Sex Tourism and Public Health
- Tips to Avoid Being Solicited
- Law of the Land Hypothetical
- Takeaways

PROSTITUTION

Overview[17]

Prostitution in Germany is **legal** and sex work is seen as a **legitimate form of labor**. Those involved in prostitution have legal protections, such as the ability to work independently, sign contracts, and pay taxes. Sex workers have the **same employment rights** and social benefits as workers in other sectors, including health insurance and retirement provisions.

While **brothels are allowed to operate**, they must comply with regulations on hygiene, health, and safety. However, there are strict measures to combat trafficking and exploitation, and those found guilty of forcing individuals into sex work face severe penalties.

The root causes of prostitution in Germany are primarily socio-economic in nature. Poverty and economic inequality play a significant role, as many individuals, particularly women, turn to sex work out of financial necessity or a lack of better job opportunities. A lack of education and limited career prospects often leave individuals vulnerable to the sex industry. Gender inequality and social marginalization contribute to the overrepresentation of women in prostitution, reflecting broader societal patterns. Migrants, especially those from low-income countries, are also disproportionately involved in sex work, often due to a lack of legal

---

17   https://www.nswp.org/country/germany

employment options and the exploitation they face in precarious situations. Additionally, the demand for sex services, fueled by domestic and international sex tourism, sustains the industry in Germany, where the legal framework creates a relatively open environment for such work.

Recent regulatory trends have focused on improving the conditions for sex workers while cracking down on exploitation. The **Prostitution Act of 2017** marked a major shift by requiring registration and health checks for sex workers, making it a more formalized profession with legal protections. The law also emphasized combating human trafficking and introduced stricter penalties for trafficking offenses. Alongside this, there has been an increase in support programs to help individuals exit prostitution, offering assistance in finding education, jobs, and social services. Additionally, efforts have been made to regulate street and online sex work, with some cities designating specific areas for street prostitution to improve safety and reduce public disturbances.

Laws and Penalties[18]

Prostitution in Germany has been legal and regulated since the implementation of the **Prostitution Act** (*Prostitutionsgesetz*) in **2002**, which aimed to improve the legal status of sex workers. This act allows for licensed brothels and sex work, and the industry is subject to taxation. Furthermore, the "**Prostitute Protection Act**," enacted in **2017**, established comprehensive guidelines for the regulation and protection of sex workers, including registration requirements and health checks.

Designated areas for prostitution, known as *Sperrbezirke* (**restricted zones**), exist in many German cities. These areas are defined by local governments, and sex work is only permitted within them. Outside these zones, prostitution may be banned or limited. Regulations can vary widely between municipalities, depending on local social and political conditions.

---

18 https://www.aidshilfe.de/medien/en/md/
gesund-im-job-healthy-at-work-englisch/sex-work-and-law/

Local authorities regulate these areas through zoning laws, time restrictions, and regular police inspections. Street prostitution, for example, may only be allowed at specific times and in isolated areas. Brothels, bars, and other establishments must comply with local licensing, hygiene, and safety requirements.

Sex workers are legally required to register with local authorities and attend regular health counseling sessions—annually for adults over 21 and every six months for those under 21. They must carry a registration certificate, which can use an alias to protect their identity. They must also be **at least 18 years old**. Operators of brothels or similar establishments are required to obtain a license and are subject to regulatory oversight.

Penalties for prostitution-related infractions vary. **Working without registration** can lead to fines of up to €1,000 (about US$1,118). **Violating *Sperrbezirk* restrictions** may result in fines up to €5,000 (about US$5,590). Operating a brothel without a license or failing to follow health and safety rules can result in higher fines or criminal charges. More serious offenses, such as trafficking, coercion, or exploitation, carry severe penalties, including imprisonment.

Prostitution Practices

One of the most visible forms of prostitution in Germany is **street prostitution**. This practice involves sex workers soliciting clients in public spaces and is often subject to strict municipal control. Cities typically enforce the use of *"Sperrbezirke,"* or prohibition zones, where sex work is either entirely banned or subject to strict conditions. In some urban areas, sex workers must purchase permits or pay local taxes in order to operate legally in designated zones. Despite its legality, street prostitution remains controversial due to its visibility and perceived impact on public order, which influences the degree to which authorities restrict or facilitate its practice.

Brothels represent another significant and more institutionalized form of sex work. These establishments range from small, privately run operations to large-scale Eros centers that house multiple sex workers and offer a wide array of services. With an estimated 3,000 brothels operating across the country, this sector contributes substantially to Germany's economy.[19] The legal framework allows brothel operators to run their businesses under strict licensing and regulatory conditions, including safety measures, hygiene standards, and worker protections. This model has been praised for providing safer and more controlled working environments for sex workers, although critics argue that it can still be susceptible to exploitation and trafficking.

Escort services offer a more discreet and often higher-end form of sex work. These services typically involve sex workers meeting clients at hotels or private homes and are frequently arranged through agencies or online platforms. Escort work is generally less visible and more private than street or brothel-based prostitution, often involving higher fees and customized experiences. This segment of the industry has also expanded to include specialized services for individuals with disabilities or elderly clients, reflecting a broader social understanding of sexual needs and rights.

The rise of the internet has given way to a substantial increase in **online prostitution**. Through websites and mobile apps, sex workers can advertise services, communicate with clients, and manage appointments, offering both convenience and discretion. Online platforms have become particularly important for independent workers, allowing them greater control over their schedules and clientele. This method of sex work continues to evolve alongside digital technologies, posing new challenges for regulatory authorities attempting to monitor and protect those involved.

Despite the overarching national legal framework regarding prostitution, the enforcement of these laws is largely left to local authorities, leading to a patchwork of attitudes and practices across the country. Some municipalities adopt a more **supportive approach**, ensuring access to health services and maintaining open communication with advocacy groups. Others, influenced by conservative political or community

---

19   https://unherd.com/2022/11/germany-europes-bordello/

sentiments, may adopt **more restrictive policies**, such as aggressively policing unregistered workers, closing long-standing brothels, or enforcing tighter zoning restrictions. In some cities, attempts to implement stricter controls have met resistance from sex workers, who argue that such actions threaten their safety and livelihoods.

Sex Trafficking and Exploitation

Sex trafficking and exploitation are **significant and ongoing concerns** in Germany. The country remains a destination, source, and transit point for victims of human trafficking, particularly for the purpose of sexual exploitation. In 2022, German authorities identified over 1,500 trafficking victims, with nearly one-third of them under the age of 21 and a vast majority being women. These numbers reflect an increase compared to previous years and underline the persistent challenges in tackling this crime.

Victims often come from both within Germany and abroad, particularly from countries such as Romania, Bulgaria, Nigeria, Vietnam, and Thailand. Vulnerable individuals are typically lured through deception, coercion, or false promises of employment, with traffickers exploiting their social and economic hardships.

Certain areas of Germany are more prone to sex trafficking than others. Large urban centers such as **Berlin**, **Hamburg**, and **Frankfurt** tend to be hotspots due to the size of their sex industries, greater anonymity, and higher demand. These cities also attract international populations, which can include undocumented migrants and asylum seekers who are especially vulnerable to exploitation due to their precarious legal or financial status. Additionally, regions with high numbers of migrant laborers and insufficient local oversight can become breeding grounds for trafficking operations.

Young women, **teenagers**, and **undocumented migrants** represent the demographics most at risk of being trafficked for sexual purposes. Many are manipulated into exploitative situations through romantic relationships or job offers, while others are abducted or sold by criminal networks. Victims are often isolated, kept under surveillance, and threatened with violence, deportation, or harm to their families to ensure compliance.

In response, the German government has taken a number of measures to address sex trafficking and exploitation. In 2016, it enacted the **Act to Improve Action Against Human Trafficking**, aligning national laws with European Union directives and expanding the definition of trafficking to include broader forms of coercion and control. The government has also developed national action plans to combat labor exploitation and forced labor and has worked to improve coordination between law enforcement, social services, and non-governmental organizations. One key partner is the NGO network **KOK**, Network and Coordination Office Against Trafficking In Human Beings, which received over half a million euros in funding in 2022 to support victim assistance and advocacy programs.[20] Germany also engages in international cooperation with other European nations and organizations such as EUROPOL to carry out joint operations targeting trafficking networks.

Despite these efforts, significant challenges remain, including the identification of victims, securing their cooperation with authorities, and ensuring long-term support and protection. Continued investment in prevention, education, and victim-centered approaches is essential to effectively combat sex trafficking and exploitation across Germany.

 ## Sex Tourism and Public Health

Sex tourism is **relatively well-developed** in Germany, primarily due to the country's legal and regulated framework for prostitution. This legal environment allows sex work to operate openly and professionally, attracting both domestic and international clients seeking sexual services in a controlled setting.

---

20 https://www.lastradainternational.org/kok/

The development of sex tourism in Germany is further supported by the existence of large, well-known brothels and red-light districts in cities like **Hamburg (Reeperbahn)**, **Cologne (Pascha, Europe's largest brothel)**, **Frankfurt**, and **Berlin**. These areas offer a wide range of services and are easily accessible, with infrastructure that supports tourism more generally like hotels, nightlife, and transport.

Another key factor is the perception of **safety** and **hygiene**. Germany mandates regular health checks and the use of condoms, creating an environment that many tourists see as safer compared to countries where prostitution is illegal or less regulated. Additionally, services are often advertised transparently through websites and travel forums, making it easier for sex tourists to plan visits.

Economic factors also play a role. Sex tourism contributes to local economies, and the industry is supported by a network of legal businesses including clubs, escort services, and accommodations that cater to adult tourism. However, this development is not without controversy, as concerns about human trafficking, exploitation, and public health persist despite the regulatory framework.

Tips to Avoid Being Solicited

If you're visiting Germany and want to avoid being solicited by sex workers—especially in areas where prostitution is legal and visible—here are some practical tips to help you steer clear of unwanted approaches:

- Stay away from areas that are known for legalized sex work. These neighborhoods often have clubs, bars, and brothels where soliciting can occur openly.

- In some areas, sex workers may approach individuals who appear to be tourists, especially solo males. Dressing modestly, avoiding lingering in red-light areas, and walking with purpose can reduce the chances of being approached.

- If you're out at night, stick to busy public areas and avoid alleyways or back streets where street-based sex work is more likely to happen. This also adds a layer of safety in general.

- If someone approaches you, a simple "No, thank you" or shaking your head and walking away is usually enough. Most sex workers in Germany are professional and will not persist if you clearly show you're not interested.

- Solo travelers, especially men, are more likely to be approached. Being with friends or a partner often deters soliciting and gives you backup if someone is persistent.

 **Law of the Land Hypothetical**

HYPOTHETICAL: *Liam, a 34-year-old tourist from Ireland, is visiting Berlin and unknowingly walks into a red-light district. He's approached by a woman offering sexual services for €100 (about US$110). He agrees and goes with her to a nearby apartment. Afterward, she demands €200 (about US$220) instead, threatening to call the police if he refuses. Is it legal for the sex worker to change the price after the service, and could Liam have done anything?*

ANSWER: ***No.** Under German law, prostitution is legal and treated as a service contract. Changing the price afterward—especially under threat—could be considered fraud or extortion. Liam was within his rights to refuse and could have contacted the police. To avoid such issues, it's best to confirm terms clearly in advance and use licensed establishments, where rules and protections are enforced.*

Takeaways

- Prostitution is **legal** and **regulated**, with sex work treated as a profession. Laws like the 2002 Prostitution Act and 2017 Protection Act ensure worker rights, registration, and health checks.

- **Strict zoning and licensing laws apply**, including *Sperrbezirke* (restricted zones). Sex work is only allowed in designated areas, and brothels must meet legal standards for hygiene and safety.

- Forms of prostitution vary, from street work and brothels to escort services and online platforms. Each comes with different levels of visibility, regulation, and risk.

- Sex trafficking is a major concern, especially involving young women, minors, and migrants. Despite strong laws, challenges remain in identifying and supporting victims.

- Sex tourism is common, particularly in major cities. While the legal framework attracts clients, it also raises concerns about exploitation and public health.

LGBTQ

LGBTQ

Homophobia in Germany

Germany's relationship with its LGBTQ+ community has evolved significantly over time. Historically, Germany was once at the forefront of LGBTQ+ advocacy, particularly in the early 20th century, when Berlin was considered a hub for gay culture and research. This progressive atmosphere was shattered during the Nazi era, when **homosexuality— especially among men—was criminalized under Paragraph 175**, and thousands were persecuted. After World War II, anti-homosexuality laws remained in place in West Germany until partial decriminalization in 1969 and full repeal in 1994. In recent decades, Germany has made major legal and cultural strides in support of LGBTQ+ rights.

Today, the general cultural attitude in Germany is largely supportive of LGBTQ+ individuals, particularly in urban centers like Berlin, Hamburg, and Cologne. A 2019 Eurobarometer survey found that 88 percent of Germans support equal rights for LGBTQ+ people, and 84% percent support same-sex marriage. However, acceptance can vary by region, with rural areas and parts of the former East Germany sometimes exhibiting more conservative views.

Cultural and social factors such as education, generational differences, and religious beliefs continue to influence attitudes. While many Protestant churches in Germany bless same-sex unions, the Catholic Church remains divided, with some dioceses defying Vatican guidance to offer blessings. Broader societal values around individual freedom and secularism have generally fostered more acceptance.

Despite legal protections, **homophobia and transphobia still manifest in daily life.** In workplaces, over 30 percent of LGBTQ+ people report discrimination or harassment, leading many to hide their identity. In schools, LGBTQ+ students often face bullying, and in family settings, especially more traditional households, some individuals experience rejection or pressure to conform. Public attitudes have improved, but subtle forms of discrimination persist and there are still reported cases of violence and hate crimes against LGBTQ+ individuals. These incidents range from verbal abuse to physical violence, often occurring in nightlife areas or during public demonstrations.

Germany has several high-profile figures who openly support LGBTQ+ rights. **Former Berlin mayor Klaus Wowereit** was one of the first openly gay major politicians in the country, famously stating, "*Ich bin schwul – und das ist auch gut so*" ("I am gay – and that's a good thing"). Other advocates include former **Foreign Minister Guido Westerwelle** and current political figures like **Health Minister Jens Spahn**. These and other public figures have significantly contributed to the LGBTQ+ cause in Germany by using their platforms to promote visibility, challenge stereotypes, and advocate for equal rights. Their openness about their sexuality has helped normalize LGBTQ+ representation in politics and public life. By holding high-profile positions, they have influenced policies related to LGBTQ+ rights and provided role models for the community, showing that being openly LGBTQ+ does not limit success or acceptance. Their work has also paved the way for greater dialogue and progress on issues like same-sex marriage, anti-discrimination laws, and LGBTQ+ inclusion in society.

LGBTQ Legislation

Over the past decade, Germany has enacted significant legislation and initiatives that underscore its commitment to LGBTQ+ rights and recognition. These developments reflect a societal shift toward greater equality, protection, and visibility for LGBTQ+ individuals. Some of these include:

- **Legalization of Same-Sex Marriage (2017):** In June 2017, Germany's parliament passed a law legalizing same-sex marriage, with the legislation coming into effect on October 1, 2017. This law granted same-sex couples the same legal rights as heterosexual couples, including the right to marry and adopt children. The passage of this law was a significant milestone in the global movement toward marriage equality.[21]

- **Ban on Conversion Therapy for Minors (2020):** In May 2020, Germany enacted legislation banning so-called "conversion therapy" for minors. The law criminalizes practices aimed at changing or suppressing an individual's sexual orientation or gender identity, including advertising such services. Violations can result in fines or imprisonment. This legislation reflects a commitment to protecting minors from harmful and discredited practices.[22] (See Law of the Land True Story below)

- **Passage of the Self-Determination Act (2024):** In April 2024, Germany's parliament passed the Selbstbestimmungsgesetz (Self-Determination Act), allowing individuals aged 16 and over to change their legal gender and first name through a simple administrative process based on self-identification. This law replaced the previous requirements, which included medical assessments and court rulings, reflecting a more progressive approach to gender recognition.[23]

- **Compensation for Victims of Nazi-Era Anti-Gay Laws (2021):** In 2021, Germany began compensating individuals persecuted under Paragraph 175, the Nazi-era law that criminalized homosexuality between men. The compensation includes financial payments and reflects a societal acknowledgment of past injustices.[24]

---

21 https://www.washingtonpost.com/world/germanys-parliament-legalizes-same-sex-marriage-bringing-it-in-line-with-most-neighbors

22 https://www.bbc.com/news/world-europe-52585162?utm_source

23 https://en.wikipedia.org/wiki/Gender_self-identification

24 https://www.them.us/story/germany-compensates-lgbtq-people-persecuted-under-nazi-era-anti-gay-law

Collectively, these laws reflect Germany's ongoing efforts to promote equality, protect individuals from discrimination, and acknowledge historical wrongs. However, the rise in hate crimes indicates that legislative progress must be accompanied by continuous societal and cultural efforts to achieve full acceptance and equality for LGBTQ+ individuals.

LGBTQ Tourism and Safety Concerns

LGBTQ+ tourism is **well-developed** in Germany, supported by a progressive legal framework and a vibrant gay cultural scene. Major cities such as Berlin, Cologne, Hamburg, and Munich are known for their LGBTQ+-friendly environments, hosting **Pride events**, **gay film festivals**, and **inclusive nightlife**. Berlin, in particular, is recognized globally as a top LGBTQ+ destination due to its open-minded atmosphere, historical significance, and diverse community.

Tolerance toward the LGBTQ community can vary depending on the region. Urban centers generally embrace diversity and inclusion, while more conservative or rural areas may be less accepting, though outright hostility is relatively uncommon. Cities like Berlin and Cologne are celebrated for their inclusivity, whereas parts of Bavaria or eastern Germany might exhibit more traditional attitudes.

Public displays of affection between LGBTQ+ individuals are **generally acceptable** in Germany, especially in larger cities. Kissing, holding hands, or other gestures of affection between same-sex couples are commonly seen in public and are usually met with indifference or support. However, in some rural or conservative areas, such displays might draw attention or disapproval, so discretion is occasionally advised based on context.

In terms of safety, **Germany is broadly considered safe for LGBTQ+ visitors**. Legal protections exist against discrimination and hate crimes, and most travelers experience no issues. That said, incidents of homophobic or transphobic harassment, while relatively rare, do occur, particularly in nightlife settings or during large public events. As with any destination, being aware of your surroundings and local social cues can help ensure a positive and safe experience.

 ## General Questions

1. *Do laws in Germany protect homosexual expressions and conduct?* **Yes.** Laws in Germany do protect homosexual expressions and conduct. Same-sex relationships are legal, and Germany has enacted several laws to safeguard the rights of LGBTQ+ individuals. These include anti-discrimination protections under the **General Equal Treatment Act, the legalization of same-sex marriage in 2017**, and the **recognition of same-sex adoption rights.** Public expressions of affection between same-sex partners are legal and generally accepted, particularly in urban areas. Hate speech or violence based on sexual orientation is also punishable under German criminal law.

2. *Are transgender individuals legally recognized and protected in Germany?* **Yes.** Transgender individuals are legally recognized and increasingly protected in Germany. As of 2024, the **Self-Determination Act** allows people aged 16 and older to change their legal gender and name through a simple administrative declaration, without needing medical or psychological evaluations. This marks a significant step forward in affirming trans rights. Additionally, anti-discrimination laws protect transgender individuals in areas such as employment, education, and access to services. While social challenges remain, especially in rural areas, legal progress reflects growing recognition and support for transgender rights in Germany.

Law of the Land True Story

In May 2020, Germany passed a landmark law banning so-called "conversion therapy" for minors, aiming to protect young people from harmful practices that claim to change a person's sexual orientation or gender identity. The legislation prohibits anyone under 18 from undergoing medical or psychological interventions intended to suppress or alter their LGBTQ+ identity. Violators can face up to one year in prison or a fine of up to €30,000 (about US$32,535).

Health Minister Jens Spahn, who is openly gay, spearheaded the bill, emphasizing the need for clear legal protections, especially for minors who are often coerced or misled into such treatments. He described the law as a message of support and validation for LGBTQ+ youth. The ban also holds parents and guardians accountable if they force children into conversion therapy using threats or deceit.

While the move was widely praised, some critics argued it didn't go far enough, calling for the age limit to be extended to include young adults. Still, the law marked an important step in affirming the dignity and rights of LGBTQ+ individuals in Germany and aligns the country with others taking similar actions to outlaw the practice.

Law of the Land Hypothetical

HYPOTHETICAL: *Jamie, a transgender woman from the United States, travels to Germany for a work conference. At the airport, security stops her because her gender marker on her passport doesn't match her gender presentation. The staff expresses confusion and suggests she may not be allowed to pass without additional proof of her identity. Does Jamie have legal protections against discrimination at the airport, and how should she handle the situation?*

ANSWER: *Yes. Jamie is protected by Germany's **General Equal Treatment Act (AGG)**, which prohibits discrimination based on gender* *identity in all public spaces, including airports. If she feels discriminated against, she can file a complaint with the Anti-Discrimination Agency of Germany (ADS). While there may be confusion, the staff should respect her gender identity. Jamie has the right to calmly explain the situation, and if mistreated, she can seek legal recourse. German law mandates respect for transgender individuals in public services.*

CHAPTER 9

SEXUALLY MOTIVATED/ VIOLENT CRIMES

IN THIS CHAPTER

- Overview
- Related Legislation
- General Questions
- Law of the Land Hypothetical
- Takeaways

SEXUALLY MOTIVATED/ VIOLENT CRIMES

Overview

Sexually motivated crimes in Germany, like in many other countries, are a significant concern for law enforcement and the public. While the country has made substantial strides in addressing these crimes, they remain a prevalent issue, often influenced by various social, cultural, and economic factors.

Germany consistently reports thousands of sexual offenses annually. For example, in 2021, there were over 8,000 reported cases of rape and sexual assault, according to official crime statistics from the German Federal Criminal Police Office (BKA). These crimes encompass a range of offenses, including **rape**, **sexual harassment**, **exploitation**, and **trafficking**, and their frequency has been a subject of national debate. However, many experts believe that the actual number of sexual offenses may be higher due to underreporting, especially in cases involving victims who are afraid to come forward, such as those in abusive relationships or those impacted by fear of social stigma.

Several social, cultural, and economic factors contribute to the prevalence of sexually motivated crimes. Gender inequality and entrenched traditional gender roles are often seen as significant contributors. In some cases, societal norms that objectify women and normalize sexual aggression may foster environments where such crimes are more likely to occur. Economic factors, such as poverty and social marginalization, can also leave vulnerable individuals—especially women, children, and migrants—at higher risk of exploitation or assault. Additionally, the rise of online platforms has led to concerns about the sexual exploitation of minors and the increasing phenomenon of online sexual abuse.

Women and **children**, particularly those from **marginalized communities**, are most affected by sexually motivated crimes. Victims of sexual violence often experience long-term psychological trauma, and women are disproportionately affected by rape and sexual harassment, both in public and private spheres. Young people, especially those in unstable living conditions or vulnerable environments, also face a higher risk of sexual abuse.

Regional differences in the occurrence and reporting of sexually motivated crimes in Germany do exist. Larger urban centers such as Berlin, Hamburg, and Frankfurt tend to report higher numbers of sexual offenses, which could be attributed to both the larger population and the anonymity afforded by city living. These areas also have higher numbers of marginalized groups, including migrants, who may be more vulnerable to exploitation. Conversely, rural areas might see fewer reported cases, though this may reflect lower reporting rates rather than a true lack of incidents.

Related Legislation

Sexually motivated crimes remain a serious concern in Germany, affecting a wide range of populations and sparking ongoing legal and social responses. Annually, between 7,000 and 8,000 rape cases are reported to police, but research suggests that only about 5 percent of women who experience rape report the crime, and only 13 percent of reported cases lead to a conviction. For children and adolescents, the problem is especially widespread. Although approximately 15,500 cases of child sexual abuse were reported in 2022, the World Health Organization estimates that as many as one million young people in Germany have experienced sexual violence by adults.[25]

Contributing factors include persistent gender inequality, economic hardship, and challenges related to migration and integration. Social attitudes that tolerate or normalize certain forms of aggression can also play a role. A controversial but notable trend is the growing proportion of foreign nationals among those suspected of committing sexual offenses, which rose from 35 percent in 2000 to 42 percent in 2020, particularly among nationals from Turkey, Afghanistan, and Syria.[26]

The populations most affected include **women, children**, and **marginalized groups** such as migrants, LGBTQ+ individuals, and people with disabilities. Studies show that girls are about twice as likely as boys to be affected by child sexual abuse.

There are **also regional disparities** in how often these crimes occur. Urban centers such as Berlin, Hamburg, and Munich report higher rates, likely due to population density and anonymity. Transportation hubs are another hotspot. In train stations and on trains, foreign nationals—who make up about 15 percent of the population—are reported to commit 59 percent of sexual crimes. Overall sexual violence in Berlin alone increased by 260 percent since 2013.[27]

In light of these issues, Germany has continued to strengthen legal protections, enhance victim services, and raise public awareness through education and prevention initiatives. However, underreporting, social stigma, and difficulties in prosecution remain significant challenges in the fight against sexually motivated crimes.

25 https://beauftragte-missbrauch.de/en/themen/definition/
    figures-on-child-sexual-abuse-in-germany

26 https://europeanconservative.com/articles/news/germany-past-2-de-
    cades-saw-proportion-of-foreign-sex-offenders-rise-dramatically

27 https://rmx.news/article/germany-foreigners-commit-59-of-all-sexual-
    crimes-in-trains-and-train-stations-sexual-crimes-double-since-2019/

General Questions

1. ***Do laws in Germany related to sex crimes protect the victims equally?*** **Yes.** Germany's sex crime laws are designed to protect all victims equally, regardless of gender, nationality, or sexual orientation. Key reforms, like the **2016 "No means No" law**, made it easier to prosecute non-consensual acts even without physical resistance. While the legal framework is victim-centered and neutral, practical challenges like underreporting, evidence issues, and unequal access to support can lead to disparities in protection—especially for marginalized groups such as migrants, LGBTQ+ individuals, and people with disabilities.

2. ***Pursuant to law, what is the age of consent for sex in Germany?*** In Germany, the **age of consent is 14**. However, if the older partner is over 21, sex is only legal if there's no exploitation or abuse of the younger person's lack of understanding. Sex with anyone under 14 is always illegal, and special rules apply to protect teens from authority figures like teachers.

Law of the Land Hypothetical

HYPOTHETICAL: *John, a 28-year-old American tourist in Berlin, is groped by a man at a tram stop. Despite expressing discomfort, the man continues his behavior. John leaves the area and reports the incident to the police, providing a description of the man. What should John do to ensure the harassment is addressed under German law, and what protections are available to him?*

ANSWER: *John should report the harassment to the nearest police station or call **110**. Sexual harassment is a punishable offense under German law, and as a foreigner, John is equally protected. He should provide all* *details, including the description of the perpetrator and any evidence. John can also seek support from victim organizations like Weißer Ring and request translation services if needed. By taking these steps, John can ensure the incident is investigated and appropriate action is taken.*

 **Takeaways**

- Sexual offenses like rape and harassment continue to be widespread in Germany, though many go unreported, especially among vulnerable groups.

- Gender inequality and traditional social norms contribute significantly to the prevalence of sexual crimes, with women, children, and migrants being most affected.

- Germany's legal reforms have made it easier to prosecute non-consensual acts, though challenges like underreporting and unequal access to support persist.

- Larger cities like Berlin and Hamburg report more sexual offenses due to higher population density and anonymity, while rural areas often see fewer reported cases.

- In Germany, the legal age of consent is 14, with additional protections against exploitation, particularly for minors and vulnerable individuals, including those in relationships with authority figures.

ARRESTED IN GERMANY

CHAPTER 10
ARRESTED IN GERMANY

Overview

When traveling in a foreign country, it's imperative to recognize that you are subject to the legal jurisdiction and regulations of that nation. These laws may significantly differ from those in your home country and might not offer the same legal protections you are accustomed to. It's crucial to bear in mind that penalties for violating foreign laws can be more severe than those for similar offenses in your home country, and ignorance of these laws is not typically accepted as a defense.

The consequences for breaking the law while abroad can be severe and may include expulsion, fines, arrest, or imprisonment. Even unintentional violations can lead to serious legal repercussions. It is essential for travelers to be aware of and adhere to the laws of the host country to avoid legal entanglements and ensure a safe and enjoyable experience.

Specifically, stringent penalties are often enforced for possession, use, or trafficking of illegal drugs in many countries. Convicted offenders can expect severe consequences, including lengthy jail sentences and hefty fines. The legal processes for foreigners in the event of an arrest abroad involve being charged or indicted, prosecuted, potentially convicted and sentenced, and, if applicable, going through an appeals process.

Navigating a foreign legal system can be complex, and individuals arrested abroad must be prepared to comply with the legal procedures of the host country. Seeking legal representation and understanding the local legal nuances are crucial steps for those facing legal issues in a foreign jurisdiction.

Awareness of and adherence to the laws of a foreign country are paramount when traveling. Understanding the potential consequences for legal violations and being prepared to navigate the legal system of the host country are essential aspects of responsible international travel.

Arrest Process

In Germany, the arrest process follows a structured legal framework designed to protect individual rights while allowing law enforcement to investigate suspected criminal behavior. Arrests typically occur when the police have reasonable suspicion that a person has committed a crime. Common criminal charges include **theft, assault, drug offenses, fraud, driving under the influence, sexual offenses**, and **immigration-related violations**. Theft and assault are among the most frequent, while drug-related crimes and fraud often carry more serious penalties, especially if organized or repeated.

When someone is arrested, they are informed of the reason for their detention and of their rights, including the right to remain silent and the right to contact a lawyer. If the arrested individual is a foreigner, they are also informed of their right to contact their embassy or consulate. The language used during this process must be one the person understands, and an interpreter is provided if necessary.

The police may initially hold a person for **up to 24 to 48 hours**. Within that time, a judge must review the arrest and determine whether the individual should be released or placed in **pre-trial detention**. Pre-trial detention, or Untersuchungshaft, is typically reserved for serious offenses or when there is a risk that the suspect might flee, tamper with evidence, or commit further crimes.

After the arrest, the public prosecutor begins a **preliminary investigation**. If enough evidence is gathered, formal charges are filed. If not, the case may be dropped or resolved through alternative measures like fines or community service. If charges are brought forward, the case proceeds to trial, where both the defense and prosecution present evidence and call witnesses. Trials vary in complexity depending on the nature of the crime, with more serious offenses involving more formal court proceedings. If found guilty, the accused may receive penalties ranging from fines and probation to imprisonment. Appeals are allowed and can be submitted to higher courts for review.

For foreigners, a criminal conviction can have additional consequences, such as **revocation of residency permits** or **deportation**, especially in cases involving serious crimes or repeat offenses. Non-EU citizens are more vulnerable to immigration-related penalties than EU nationals, who generally enjoy greater legal protections under freedom of movement laws.

Throughout the process, Germany emphasizes **due process**, **legal representation**, and the **right to a fair trial**. However, for foreigners unfamiliar with the legal system or language, navigating the process can be particularly challenging, making access to legal counsel and consular support crucial.

Rights of the Arrested Person[28]

In Germany, the rights of an arrested person are protected under the **German Constitution** (*Grundgesetz*) and the **Code of Criminal Procedure** (*Strafprozessordnung – StPO*). These rights, intended to ensure due process and fair treatment during criminal proceedings, include:

- **Right to Be Informed of the Arrest and Charges:** An arrested person must be promptly informed that they are under arrest, the reason for their arrest, and the specific criminal offense they are being accused of. This information must be communicated in a language they understand, and if necessary, an interpreter must be provided

---

28 https://www.gov.uk/guidance/arrested-or-in-prison-in-germany)

to ensure clear and accurate understanding of the situation and their rights.

- **Right to Remain Silent (Schweigerecht):** The suspect has the right to remain silent and cannot be forced to answer questions. This is similar to the "Miranda right" in the U.S.

- **Right to Legal Counsel (Recht auf einen Anwalt):** The person has the right to consult a lawyer **immediately**, even before the first police questioning. In serious cases, or if the person is in pre-trial detention, a public defender (*Pflichtverteidiger*) may be assigned.

- **Right to Notify a Third Party:** The arrested person can request that a relative or another trusted person be informed about the arrest. **Foreign nationals** have the right to **contact their consulate or embassy**.

- **Right to an Interpreter:** If the arrested person does not speak German, they have the right to a **qualified interpreter** at all stages (police questioning, court proceedings, and during communication with their lawyer).

- **Right to Judicial Review (Richtervorführung):** A person cannot be held by the police for more than **48 hours** without being brought before a judge. The judge decides whether the arrest was legal and if the person should be released or placed in **pre-trial detention** (*Untersuchungshaft*).

- **Right to Review of Detention:** If placed in custody, the suspect can **appeal** the detention and ask for a review by a higher court.

- **Protection from Mistreatment:** The person has the right to be treated **with dignity and without coercion or abuse**. Evidence obtained through mistreatment or torture is **inadmissible** in court.

- **Right to Access Case Files (via a lawyer):** Once represented by a lawyer, the defense has the right to **inspect the case files** to know what evidence has been collected.

These rights are fundamental and must be upheld throughout the criminal process. Any violation—especially denial of legal counsel or interpretation—can lead to procedural issues that may impact the legality of the arrest or trial.

Getting Legal Assistance

One of the most crucial rights when detained in Germany is the accused's right to legal counsel, meaning that **an arrested person has the immediate right to consult with a lawyer, receive legal advice, and have a defense attorney present during police questioning and throughout the criminal proceedings.** This right in Germany extends to **non-citizens** and **visitors** as well. Regardless of nationality, anyone who is arrested in Germany has the right to consult with a lawyer, receive legal representation, and be advised of their legal rights during questioning and trial. Foreign nationals also have the right to an interpreter if they do not understand German. Moreover, if a foreigner is arrested, they are entitled to contact their embassy or consulate, and this right is particularly important in ensuring they have access to legal support and assistance from their home country.

An **embassy** or **consulate** can be a crucial point of contact for foreigners who encounter legal issues while traveling in another country. If a traveler is arrested, involved in a car accident, or requires medical assistance, the embassy can provide support by offering legal guidance, financial assistance, and helping to establish contact with the traveler's family and home country authorities. While embassies **do not provide direct legal representation**, they can assist in finding local attorneys and ensuring the individual's rights are protected under local law.

 American citizens may choose to notify the U.S. Embassy or consulate of the arrest using the *American Citizens Services Contact Form* **https://de.usembassy.gov/contact/**

They can help contact family, friends, or employers of the detained U.S. citizen with their written consent, visit the detained U.S. citizen in jail, help ensure that prison officials provide appropriate medical care, explain the local criminal justice and legal processes, and most importantly, connect you to local attorneys who speak English.[29] Bear in mind,

---

29 https://de.usembassy.gov/services/

their powers are limited and they cannot get U.S. citizens out of jail, provide legal advice or represent U.S. citizens in court, serve as official interpreters or translators, nor can they pay your legal, medical, or other fees.

U.S. Embassy in Berlin

Clayallee 170, 14191 Berlin
Phone: +(49) (30) 8305-0
Website: https://de.usembassy.gov/

Bail[30]

Germany does not have a bail system like in some other countries, such as the United States. Instead, the German legal system uses **pre-trial detention** (*Untersuchungshaft*) and **conditional release**, referred to as "*Kaution*" or "*Sicherheitsleistung*," both meaning "security deposit."

When a person is arrested in Germany, the public prosecutor may request that the individual be placed in pre-trial detention, which is usually reserved for cases where there is a strong suspicion of a serious crime, a risk of flight, or concerns that the person might tamper with evidence. Pre-trial detention can last for an extended period, but the court must review it regularly to ensure that it remains justified.

However, there are alternatives to pre-trial detention, such as **conditional release**. This means that a person might be released under specific conditions, such as:

- Surrendering their passport or travel documents.
- Agreeing to report regularly to the police.
- Providing a financial guarantee (similar to bail in some countries, though this is rare and more restrictive than typical bail practices).

---

30 https://se-legal.de/criminal-defense-lawyer/bail-in-germany/?lang=en

Foreigners and visitors are **eligible for conditional release**, just like German citizens. However, the decision to grant release, and the conditions imposed, often depend on the individual's risk of fleeing the country, the seriousness of the offense, and the likelihood of the person adhering to the conditions set by the court. Foreign nationals may face stricter conditions, such as the possibility of being required to remain in the country until the trial or investigation is concluded.

Complaints Against Police

The police force in Germany is generally regarded as **professional, well-trained**, and **effective** in enforcing the law. Most Germans have a high level of trust in their police, especially when it comes to maintaining public order and safety. The police are seen as competent in handling crime, emergencies, and public events. However, like in many countries, the reputation of the police can vary depending on the region and the specific actions of individual officers.

The most common complaints against the German police include the **excessive use of force**, particularly during arrests or public demonstrations, and **allegations of racial profiling or discriminatory behavior** toward ethnic minorities and foreigners. Some individuals report mistreatment during detention or a lack of respect for legal rights, such as not being properly informed of their rights upon arrest. There are also concerns about the **inadequate investigation** of misconduct complaints and occasional accusations of corruption or abuse of power. While these issues are not widespread, they have prompted calls for greater transparency, independent oversight, and improved accountability within the police force.

To file a **complaint against the police** in Germany, you can start by contacting the **local police station** where the incident occurred, either in person, by phone, or in writing. If the complaint involves serious misconduct, you may also report it directly to the **public prosecutor's office**, which can initiate an investigation. In some federal states, there are **independent police ombudsmen** who handle complaints against law enforcement officers and ensure impartial review. Larger cities may offer online platforms for submitting complaints as well. In cases involving human rights concerns, especially discrimination or abuse, individuals can also seek help from **national human rights institutions** or **civil rights non-government organizations** (NGOs) that provide legal advice and advocacy throughout the complaint process.

There are several NGOs and human rights organizations that offer support to individuals filing complaints against the police in Germany, especially in cases of abuse, racial discrimination, or human rights violations. These organizations can provide legal advice, advocacy, and help guide you through the complaint process. The major NGOs in Germany that can help with police complaints and related legal issues are **Amnesty International Germany**, which advocates for human rights and investigates police misconduct; the **German Institute for Human Rights**, which monitors human rights protections and offers guidance in cases involving law enforcement; **Pro Asyl**, which supports refugees and migrants, especially in situations involving police mistreatment or discrimination; and the **Federal Anti-Discrimination Agency**, which assists individuals facing discrimination, including racial profiling by police.

 **General Questions**

1. *If I am convicted in Germany, am I likely to be conditionally released pending the outcome of my appeal?* In Germany, you are not automatically released after a conviction while your appeal is pending. Release depends on factors like flight risk, seriousness of the offense, and ties to Germany. Courts may allow conditional release, but it's not guaranteed—especially for foreigners.

2. *What influences a bail determination?* In Germany, bail-like conditional release is influenced by factors such as the severity of the offense, the strength of the evidence, the suspect's criminal history, risk of fleeing, potential to tamper with evidence or influence witnesses, and ties to the country, like residence, job, or family. Foreign nationals may face stricter conditions due to a higher perceived flight risk.

3. *Who is entitled to conditional release?* In Germany, anyone under investigation or awaiting trial may be entitled to conditional release, regardless of nationality, as long as they are not considered a flight risk, a danger to the public, or likely to interfere with the investigation. The court assesses each case individually, and if the conditions for pre-trial detention aren't met, release with certain restrictions may be granted.

4. *If I am arrested, how soon will I see a judge or magistrate?* If you are arrested in Germany, you must be brought before a judge **within 48 hours**. The judge will review the arrest, inform you of the charges, and decide whether to release you or place you in pre-trial detention.

5. *Will I be able to contact my country's embassy in Germany?* **Yes.** If you are arrested in Germany, you have the right to contact your country's embassy or consulate. German authorities are required to inform you of this right, and, upon request, they must notify your embassy without delay.

JAILS VS. PRISONS: CONDITIONS & CULTURE

JAILS VS. PRISONS: CONDITIONS & CULTURE

Overview[31]

In Germany's criminal justice system, the distinction between jails and prisons is less pronounced than in some other countries, but generally, **jails** (*Untersuchungshaftanstalten*) refer to facilities that hold individuals in **pre-trial detention or short-term custody**, while **prisons** (*Justizvollzugsanstalten* or JVAs) are for those serving **sentenced terms**. Jails primarily house individuals who are awaiting trial or sentencing and are generally smaller with tighter restrictions, while prisons are designed for longer stays and are structured to support reintegration through rehabilitation programs.

German jails and prisons are operated by the individual **federal states** (*Länder*) rather than by the national government, which means that while there is a consistent legal framework set by federal law, the administration, facilities, and available programs can vary by region. Staff are trained professionals, and facilities are overseen by state ministries of justice.

---

31 https://www.vera.org/news/dispatches-from-germany/
what-german-prisons-do-differently

The biggest challenges facing the prison system include **overcrowding** in some regions, especially in urban areas, and **rising numbers of foreign inmates**, which can strain language and integration services. There are also ongoing concerns about **mental health care**, the availability of **qualified staff**, and the management of **radicalization** within the prison population.

Prisons in Germany are known for emphasizing **humane treatment**, **individual dignity**, and **rehabilitation** rather than punishment alone. Rehabilitation especially plays a central role in Germany's approach to incarceration. Inmates have access to a range of programs aimed at preparing them for life after release. These include **vocational training**, **education courses**, **therapy and counseling**, **addiction treatment**, and **work programs**. In many cases, prisoners are encouraged to maintain social ties and may be allowed **day release** (*Freigang*) to work or attend education outside the facility. The overall goal is to reduce recidivism by supporting reintegration into society.

Prison Conditions and Living Environment

Prisons in Germany are categorized into different **security levels**, which determine the type of housing and restrictions placed on inmates. The classification system generally includes:

- **Minimum-security units** are for inmates with lower risks of escape or violence. These units often allow more freedom of movement and have fewer restrictions.

- **Medium-security units** house individuals who may pose a higher risk but still allow for a fair amount of freedom in comparison to high-security units.

- **Maximum-security units** are designed for those who pose significant risks, either due to the severity of their crimes, the likelihood of escape, or violent behavior.

Inmates are classified based on their **criminal history**, the **nature of their crime**, the **risk they pose**, and their **behavior** while incarcerated. This system allows for personalized management, where inmates are placed in facilities that suit their security needs, providing the appropriate level of supervision and control.

In Germany, prisoners are entitled to **adequate medical care**, which is **mandated by law**. This includes access to general health services, **mental health care**, and **specialist treatments**. Every prison has a **medical facility** or **on-site doctor** to provide routine health services, and serious medical cases are referred to external hospitals when needed. However, there are some challenges, especially **with mental health care**. The prison system can sometimes struggle to address the needs of inmates suffering from mental illness, addiction, or post-traumatic stress. Access to psychiatric services is available, but with a limited number of specialists, leading to concerns about the adequacy of treatment, particularly in overcrowded or under-resourced facilities. Additionally, the **integration of foreign prisoners**—who may not speak German or have different cultural perceptions of healthcare—can also present challenges in providing adequate medical care. These barriers can delay diagnosis and treatment.

Prisoners in Germany are provided with **three meals a day**, which meet nutritional standards, ensuring they receive balanced and adequate food. Meals are typically prepared on-site, and the quality of food varies from one prison to another. In some places, inmates may have the option to participate in **kitchen work programs**, which can provide them with additional responsibilities and skills.

In terms of **sanitation**, German prisons maintain relatively high standards, with regular cleaning routines and sufficient access to hygiene facilities. Showers and toilets are provided in all cells, with the quality and privacy varying according to the security level of the unit. For example, higher-security facilities may have more restrictive conditions, while lower-security units may offer more privacy.

Basic needs, such as **clothing, bedding**, and **personal hygiene products,** are provided to inmates. In most cases, prisoners can purchase additional items from the **canteen** (prison shop), which may include items like snacks, phone cards, or hygiene products. Inmates in lower-security prisons may also be allowed to buy additional items from the outside, under strict regulations.

Inmate Rights and Legal Protections

In Germany, prisoners retain many of their constitutional rights even while incarcerated, although these rights are restricted due to the nature of their detention. They continue to be protected by fundamental rights such as the **right to human dignity, freedom from discrimination**, and **freedom of religion**. However, these rights are limited within the context of prison life. For example, prisoners have the right to communicate with family members through visits, letters, and phone calls, and they can express themselves freely, though this may be limited in cases where security and order are at risk. They are also allowed to practice their religion and participate in religious activities, and they are protected from inhumane treatment, including torture or cruel punishment, in accordance with both German law and international human rights standards. Inmates also have **the right to file complaints against any actions that violate their rights**, such as disciplinary measures or inadequate living conditions.

Prisoners in Germany have **access to legal resources** and **the right to legal representation**. They can meet privately with their lawyers, seek legal advice on issues relating to their cases or conditions, and appeal their convictions or sentences to higher courts if they believe there has been an error in the legal process. **Legal aid** is available for those who cannot afford representation, ensuring that all prisoners have access to justice. Furthermore, prisoners can request access to legal literature and case files to assist them in preparing for their defense or appeal.

While the prison system in Germany upholds standards of humane treatment, there are still concerns about potential abuse or mistreatment by prison staff or other inmates. Abuse can include physical violence, verbal mistreatment, unjustified solitary confinement, or inadequate medical care. If a prisoner experiences such abuse, they can **file complaints** with the prison administration, and these complaints are generally investigated. In some regions, prisoners can turn to an independent ombudsman to address allegations of mistreatment. If complaints are not resolved satisfactorily, prisoners have the right to take legal action against the state or prison officials, and they can also seek assistance from human rights organizations like **Amnesty International** or **Pro Asyl**. In extreme cases, prisoners may appeal to international bodies such as the **European Court of Human Rights** if their complaints of inhumane or degrading treatment are not addressed through domestic legal channels.

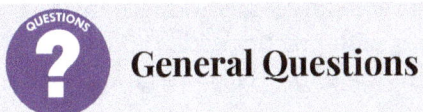

? General Questions

1. *What is the difference between a jail and prison in Germany?* In Germany, **jails** (*Untersuchungshaftanstalt*) are used for individuals awaiting trial or serving short sentences, primarily for pre-trial detention. **Prisons** (*Justizvollzugsanstalt*) house convicted individuals serving longer sentences, with facilities classified by security level. The key difference is that jails are for temporary detention, while prisons are for long-term confinement and rehabilitation.

2. *Do jails and prisons offer religious services to inmates?* **Yes**. Both jails and prisons in Germany offer religious services to inmates. Prisoners have the right to practice their religion, and facilities typically provide access to **chaplains** or religious counselors from various faiths, including Christianity, Islam, and others. Religious services, such as prayers, masses, and other spiritual activities, are regularly held, and inmates can request personal religious guidance or materials. The aim is to ensure inmates' **freedom of religion**, in line with constitutional rights.

3. *How do prisoners spend their time?* In Germany, prisoners spend their time working, studying, and participating in recreational activities. Many engage in vocational training or educational programs to develop new skills. Work programs, such as manufacturing or service tasks, are common. Inmates also have time for exercise, religious services, counseling, and social visits. These activities are designed to support rehabilitation and prepare prisoners for reintegration into society.

4. ***What type of jobs can inmates perform?*** Inmates in Germany can perform a variety of jobs within the prison, including tasks in manufacturing, craftsmanship, gardening, kitchen work, cleaning, and maintenance. Some prisons offer vocational training in fields like carpentry, metalwork, or printing. Inmates may also work in administrative roles, assisting with clerical tasks, or engage in agriculture in prisons with larger facilities. These jobs are intended to provide inmates with practical skills and a sense of responsibility, while contributing to the daily operations of the prison.

5. ***How does the prison commissary system work in Germany?*** In Germany, the **prison commissary system** (canteen) allows inmates to purchase personal items such as snacks, hygiene products, clothing, and phone cards. The commissary is typically stocked with a range of goods, including food, toiletries, writing materials, and other small necessities. Inmates can use their **personal funds** or earnings from prison work to buy items, although the selection can vary depending on the prison's resources and policies. The items available are usually modest, and purchases are subject to approval by prison authorities to maintain security and order within the facility. Some prisons also allow inmates to receive packages from family or friends, subject to certain restrictions.

6. ***What type of medical care do prisoners receive?*** Prisoners in Germany receive adequate medical care, including routine treatment, access to doctors, and referrals to external hospitals for serious conditions. Mental health services are available, though resources may be limited in some facilities. Inmates are provided with necessary medications and treatments, ensuring they receive care comparable to individuals outside the prison system.

7. *What is prison culture in Germany?* Prison culture in Germany focuses on **rehabilitation**, **order**, and **personal responsibility.** The system emphasizes education, vocational training, and therapy to help inmates reintegrate into society. While maintaining discipline, the atmosphere is less punitive, promoting individual dignity. Inmates participate in work programs, religious services, and social activities, with access to mental health support. Respect between staff and inmates is a key value, with clear rules aimed at reducing recidivism.

HELPING A FRIEND OR RELATIVE IMPRISONED IN GERMANY

HELPING A FRIEND OR RELATIVE IMPRISONED IN GERMANY

Overview

If your family member or friend is imprisoned in Germany while abroad, gather as much information as possible about their location, the charges, and the circumstances of their arrest. It is important to confirm which police station or detention center they are being held in, and whether they have access to legal representation.

You should immediately contact your **country's embassy or consulate in Germany**. The embassy can help by confirming the person's detention, providing a list of English-speaking attorneys, and helping the detainee communicate with their family. While embassies cannot interfere in the local legal process or get someone released, they can ensure fair treatment, explain local laws and procedures, and help arrange legal aid or translation services if needed.

In Germany, it is advisable to work with a local **criminal defense lawyer**, ideally one familiar with cases involving foreigners. The embassy often maintains a list of such lawyers and can make introductions if requested. It's also helpful to stay in close contact with the legal representative and ensure that any language barriers are addressed through interpreters.

German authorities are generally respectful of international legal standards, but legal processes can move slowly. Be patient, keep records of all communications, and respect German legal procedures. For further support, some NGOs or legal aid organizations (listed in the previous chapter) may also assist foreign nationals in navigating the system.

Sending Food, Supplies, and Money to an Inmate

In Germany, **sending food directly to an inmate is generally not allowed**, either by mail or during visits. Prisons provide all necessary meals, and while family and friends cannot bring cooked or packaged food, inmates can purchase additional snacks or goods through the **prison canteen**. Some exceptions may apply during holidays or special occasions, but even then, items must meet strict prison rules and usually require prior approval.

Sending packages is permitted but regulated. Packages often must be **pre-approved** by prison authorities and can only be sent a few times per year, depending on the facility's rules. Commonly allowed items include **clothing, books,** and **personal hygiene products**, though even these must meet specific guidelines. Items like **electronics, alcohol, tobacco, perishable foods,** or anything considered a security risk are **strictly prohibited**. Each prison may have slightly different rules, so it's important to check with the specific institution before sending anything.

To **send money to an inmate**, family and friends can typically **transfer funds to the prison's bank account**, referencing the inmate's name and prisoner ID number. The money is then credited to the inmate's personal account, which they can use to buy items from the canteen, phone cards, or other approved services. Transfers must comply with any prison limits on the amount and source of funds. In-person cash deposits are generally not accepted. It's important to contact the prison directly for their exact payment instructions and regulations.

Mail, Phone Calls, and Visitation

Mail

Inmates in German prisons are **allowed to receive and send mail**, and this is considered an important part of maintaining contact with the outside world. Letters are usually **inspected** by prison staff to ensure they don't contain prohibited content or pose security risks, though legal correspondence with lawyers is typically **protected and not read**. Inmates can receive letters from family, friends, and others, and they may also be allowed to send outgoing mail at their own expense. Packages, however, are subject to stricter rules and usually require prior approval.

Phone Calls

Inmates in German prisons are **not allowed to have personal cell phones**, as they are considered a security risk. All communication is regulated and monitored by prison authorities.

However, inmates are generally **allowed to make phone calls** using **designated prison telephones**, typically located in common areas. Calls are usually limited in duration, may be **monitored or recorded**, and require **prior approval**, especially for international calls. Inmates must request permission to call specific people, and the list of approved contacts is maintained by the prison.

There is no single nationwide policy on phone access, as regulations can vary by **state and facility**, but most prisons follow similar procedures. In general, prisoners are expected to pay for calls themselves using funds from their prison account. While **receiving incoming calls is not allowed**, prisoners can maintain regular contact with family and legal counsel through scheduled outgoing calls.

Visiting

Visitation in German prisons is allowed but subject to **strict rules and regulations** to ensure security and order. Generally, close family members, partners, and, in some cases, close friends are permitted to visit, but all visitors must be **pre-approved** by the prison. The inmate must submit a request with the names and details of people they wish to receive visits from, and each visitor may be required to undergo a **background check.**

The frequency and length of visits vary by prison and security level. Inmates typically receive **one to two visits per month**, with each session lasting about **30 to 60 minutes.** Higher-security prisons may impose stricter limits, while lower-security facilities may allow more frequent or longer visits. Some prisons also offer **conjugal or private family visits** under specific conditions, particularly for inmates with children or spouses.

When visiting a prison in Germany, visitors should bring **valid identification** (usually a passport or national ID) and be prepared to go through a **security screening.** Visitors are usually not allowed to bring bags, phones, or personal items into the visitation area, and physical contact may be restricted or monitored, depending on the facility's rules. Conversations are often held under supervision, and in some cases may be **recorded**, particularly for high-risk inmates.

It's important to schedule visits **well in advance**, follow dress codes, and arrive early to allow time for processing. Rules may also differ for juvenile facilities or for foreign nationals, so contacting the prison beforehand for specific guidelines is highly recommended.

Prison Scams

While Germany's prison system is tightly regulated, scams related to prisoners can still occur, particularly targeting families, friends, or good Samaritans abroad. These scams often involve false claims about a person being arrested and needing urgent money for legal fees, bail, or basic needs. Scammers may impersonate inmates, lawyers, or officials, using convincing details to pressure someone into sending money quickly—often via untraceable methods like wire transfers or gift cards.

Red flags include sudden, emotional requests for money from someone claiming to be in prison, poor grammar or vague details, pressure to act urgently, refusal to provide verifiable information, or requests to send funds to unknown third-party accounts. If someone contacts you claiming a loved one is jailed in Germany, but you've had no prior confirmation from official sources, be extremely cautious.

If you think you're being scammed, **do not send money**. Instead, contact your country's **embassy or consulate in Germany** to verify the situation. You can also reach out to the German prison or police authorities directly for confirmation. Report the scam to your local law enforcement or fraud reporting agency and save any messages or contact details as evidence. Staying informed, asking questions, and verifying everything through official channels are the best ways to protect yourself.

Upon Release

When a foreigner is released from prison in Germany, there are often specific legal consequences, depending on the nature of their offense and immigration status. In many cases, foreign nationals who are not permanent residents may face **deportation** or **removal proceedings** immediately upon release, especially if their sentence involved serious criminal offenses or if they no longer have legal grounds to stay in Germany. German immigration authorities (*Ausländerbehörde*) typically review the case before the individual is released, and in some instances, the person may be **transferred directly to immigration detention**.

Even if not deported, foreigners may be subject to **entry bans**, which can prevent them from returning to Germany—or even the entire Schengen Area—for a set period, often ranging from several years to permanently, depending on the case. Additionally, former inmates may have to **report to immigration authorities**, fulfill parole-like conditions, or comply with **supervised release terms** if applicable.

Those with legal residency or asylum status might be allowed to remain in the country but could still face **restrictions**, such as limits on movement, requirements to check in regularly with authorities, or difficulty renewing visas or permits. It's highly recommended that individuals in this situation consult with an **immigration lawyer** to understand their rights, possible legal remedies, and future options following release.

THE ADMINISTRATION
OF JUSTICE

THE ADMINISTRATION OF JUSTICE

Germany's Legal System[32]

Germany's legal system is rooted in the **civil law tradition**, heavily influenced by Roman law and codified principles developed during the 19th century. A major historical foundation is the **German Civil Code** (*Bürgerliches Gesetzbuch* or BGB), introduced in 1900, which remains central to private law today. After World War II, Germany rebuilt its legal system on democratic principles, emphasizing the rule of law, human rights, and judicial independence, enshrined in the **Basic Law** (*Grundgesetz*) of 1949, which functions as the country's constitution.

The key components of Germany's legal system include **public law**, which covers constitutional and administrative law; **criminal law**; and **private law**, which governs civil matters like contracts, family law, and property. The legal system relies on **codified statutes** rather than precedent, and judges apply these written laws to resolve disputes. Prosecutors (*Staatsanwälte*) play a central role in criminal cases, working independently but under public law guidelines.

---

32 https://www.welcome-center-germany.com/post/
navigating-the-german-legal-system-key-information

The judiciary is structured with several levels. At the base are **local and regional courts** that handle most civil and criminal cases. Above them are **higher regional courts** (*Oberlandesgerichte*) and **federal courts**, each responsible for specific areas of law. At the top are two major courts: the **Federal Court of Justice** (*Bundesgerichtshof*), which handles civil and criminal appeals, and the **Federal Constitutional Court** (*Bundesverfassungsgericht*), which ensures that laws and government actions comply with the constitution. The Constitutional Court holds significant power in reviewing legislation, protecting fundamental rights, and resolving disputes between federal and state institutions.

Unlike many countries, Germany doesn't have separate federal and state court systems, and there are no jury trials. Judges are independent and bound only by law, not by prior decisions of higher courts, though they often follow them in practice. The Federal Constitutional Court is unique in its ability to interpret the constitution and rule on the legality of laws. Additionally, German courts do not use jury trials; criminal trials are presided over by professional judges, often with the assistance of lay judges.

Despite its strengths, Germany's judiciary faces challenges, including **case backlogs**, especially in civil and immigration courts, and **resource constraints** that can delay proceedings. There's also growing debate about ensuring **equal access to justice**, particularly for non-German speakers or individuals without legal representation. Nonetheless, the system is widely respected for its structure, transparency, and adherence to the rule of law.

 **General Questions**

1. *Will the court treat first-time offenders and tourists with more leniency?* German courts often consider a person's criminal history and personal circumstances when determining sentences, so first-time offenders and tourists may receive more lenient treatment, especially for minor or non-violent offenses. Judges typically take into account factors such as intent, cooperation with authorities, expressions of remorse, and the impact of the offense. For tourists, being unfamiliar with local laws can sometimes be seen as a mitigating factor, but it does not excuse the crime. While leniency is possible, outcomes depend on the nature of the offense, the individual's behavior, and local court discretion.

2. *If I am charged with a crime, which court is likely to hear my case?* In Germany, the court that hears your case depends on the crime's severity. **Local Courts** (*Amtsgericht*) handle minor offenses, while **Regional Courts** (*Landgericht*) deal with more serious crimes. For very serious offenses like **murder** or **large-scale fraud**, the **Regional Court** is likely to be involved. Appeals or constitutional issues may be taken to **higher regional courts** or the **Federal Constitutional Court** in rare cases. The court choice is based on the crime's seriousness and legal complexity.

3. *What is the standard of proof in a criminal case in Germany?* In Germany, the **standard of proof** in a criminal case is "**beyond a reasonable doubt**" ("*Ohne vernünftigen Zweifel*"). The prosecution must present sufficient evidence to convince the court of the defendant's guilt. The **burden of proof** rests on the prosecution, and the defendant is presumed innocent until proven guilty. If there is any **reasonable doubt** about the defendant's guilt, they must be acquitted. German courts rely heavily on **written evidence** and **witness testimony**, and the judge plays an active role in gathering and evaluating the evidence, rather than relying solely on arguments from the defense and prosecution.

Law of the Land True Story[33]

In July 2024, Germany agreed to amend its constitution to further protect its Constitutional Court from potential political interference, amid growing concerns about threats to judicial independence, particularly from far-right parties. The changes were prompted by the increasing attacks on judicial systems in some Eastern European countries, like Poland, where far-right governments have undermined the separation of powers by packing courts with political appointees.

Germany's reforms aim to safeguard the court's autonomy by enshrining rules such as fixed judicial terms, age limits, and a set number of judges. The changes also introduce a mechanism to address potential vacancies in the court, preventing future political gridlocks. These constitutional amendments have broad bipartisan support across Germany's mainstream parties, signaling a strong commitment to protecting democracy and the rule of law.

Takeaways

- Germany's legal system is based on the **civil law tradition**, influenced by Roman law, and relies on **codified statutes** rather than case precedent. The German Civil Code (BGB), introduced in 1900, remains a cornerstone of private law.

- Germany's judiciary is structured in multiple levels, with **local and regional courts** handling most cases, and higher courts such as the **Federal Court of Justice** and the **Federal Constitutional Court** overseeing appeals and constitutional matters. Judges are independent and bound by law, not past decisions.

- Unlike many countries, **Germany does not use jury trials**. Criminal cases are decided by professional judges, often assisted

---

33 https://www.ft.com/content/edf420b9-fe2c-4499-a9c4-8f1de64ab743

by **lay judges**. The system emphasizes expertise and fairness over popular opinion.

- German courts may show more leniency toward **first-time offenders** and **tourists**, especially for minor offenses, taking into account factors such as intent, cooperation with authorities, and remorse. However, leniency is not guaranteed and depends on the specific circumstances.

- The standard of proof in Germany's criminal cases is "**beyond a reasonable doubt**," with the **prosecution** carrying the burden of proof. German courts rely on **written evidence** and witness testimony, with judges playing an active role in gathering and evaluating the evidence.

CRIME VICTIM ASSISTANCE

CHAPTER 14

CRIME VICTIM ASSISTANCE

Overview[34]

In Germany, crime victims have access to a wide range of resources aimed at providing physical, emotional, and legal support. Various organizations, both governmental and non-governmental, work together to ensure that victims receive timely and effective assistance. This includes information platforms, counseling services, legal aid, and compensation programs designed to address the needs of victims.

The government offers assistance through services like **victim protection offices** and the **Federal Office of Justice**, which provides **financial compensation** for victims of violent crimes under the **Crime Victims Compensation Act** (*Opferentschädigungsgesetz*). Under this act, victims of violent crime are entitled to payments in accordance if they meet certain criteria. In addition to injured parties themselves, surviving dependents such as widows and widowers as well as children and parents are entitled to payments.[35] Victims are also entitled to **legal assistance**, including support from victim advocates, especially in serious cases,

34 https://www.hilfe-info.de/Webs/hilfeinfo/EN/HelpAndAdvice/
AnsprechpartnerUndBeratungsstellen/EinrichtungenOpferhilfe/
EinrichtungenDerOpferhilfe_node.html

35 https://www.opferschutzportal.nrw/en/legal-matters/
victim-compensation-act

and can often request a **psychosocial support person** during court proceedings.

In addition to government aid, **NGOs and independent support centers** play a vital role. Organizations, such as **Weißer Ring**, offer nationwide services including counseling, legal advice, accompaniment to court, and emergency financial help.[36] Others, like **BIG Hotline** and **Frauenhauskoordinierung**, support victims of domestic violence and women in crisis. These groups often offer multilingual support and are accessible to both German citizens and foreigners.

Important **emergency contacts** in Germany include the general emergency number **112** (for police, fire, and medical emergencies) and **110** specifically for the police. Victims can also contact the **Weißer Ring Victim Hotline at 116 006**, available free of charge nationwide, while specialized hotlines are available for domestic abuse, child protection, and mental health crises.

What to Do If You Are the Victim of a Crime

If you become a victim of a crime while visiting Germany, the first step is to **ensure your safety** and then **report the incident to the police** by calling **110**, the nationwide emergency number for law enforcement. If you need urgent medical help or are in immediate danger, call **112** for emergency services. If you're injured or traumatized, go to the **nearest hospital** or seek help from a local **crisis center**. Keep all records and receipts, as you may be eligible for **compensation or insurance claims**.

After contacting the authorities, try to **document everything you can remember** about the incident, including the time, place, descriptions of people involved, and any evidence like photos or messages. If your passport or valuables were stolen, report the theft to the police and **contact your embassy or consulate** immediately for assistance with replacements and further help. Throughout the process, don't hesitate to request a **translator** or legal assistance to ensure you understand your rights and the procedures.

---

36 https://weisser-ring.de/english

You may also seek support from **victim assistance organizations**, such as **Weißer Ring**, which provide free counseling, legal guidance, and emotional support. Many of these services are available in multiple languages.

Common Tourist Scams in Germany[37]

Tourist scams in Germany, like in many major destinations, often target visitors through quick, unexpected tricks. One of the most common is **pick-pocketing**, especially in crowded areas like public transit or tourist hotspots. Tactics include the **"bump" scam**, where a thief deliberately bumps into a tourist to distract and steal from them, and the **"bird poop" scam**, where a scammer squirts a substance like mustard on a tourist and pretends to help clean it up—while picking their pockets.

Another scam involves **overly friendly locals**, who may approach tourists in bars or social spots, acting generous and engaging. They may offer to order more food or drinks, only to l**eave the tourist with the full bill** and pressure them into paying more than expected.

Taxi and train scams are also common. Some taxi drivers may **take longer routes** or **inflate prices** when they know a passenger is a tourist. On trains, fake conductors may issue **false fines** for supposed rule violations and demand immediate cash payment, which real railway staff would never do.

While most Germans are genuinely helpful and polite, **excessively friendly behavior**—especially paired with unsolicited offers or pressure—is a red flag. Tourists are advised to stay alert, trust their instincts, and not hesitate to speak up or report scams to local police. Calling attention to a scam may stop it in its tracks, and in any serious situation, contacting authorities and providing a detailed description is the best way to respond.

---

37 https://www.godigit.com/international-travel-insurance/tourist-scams/tourist-scams-in-germany

Sexual Assault

If you experience sexual assault in Germany, your safety and well-being come first. Get to a **safe place** as soon as possible and, if you're in immediate danger or need urgent medical help, call **112** for emergency services. It's strongly recommended to **report the assault to the police** by calling **110**, even if you're unsure whether to press charges. You can also go directly to a hospital or specialized crisis center (*Krisenzentrum*), where medical staff can provide urgent care and preserve evidence if you choose to report later.

When reporting the incident, you have the right to be **treated with respect and sensitivity**. You can ask for a **female officer** if you prefer and may request a **translator** if you do not speak German. Police will guide you through the process, which can include giving a statement, a medical exam, and collecting evidence. Reporting is voluntary, and victims will not be forced to proceed if they are not ready.

As a victim, you have several rights under German law: the right to **free legal advice**, the right to a **psychosocial support person** during court proceedings, and the right to **protection from the accused**, including restraining orders if needed. You are also entitled to **confidential medical care**, and in some cases, **financial compensation** through victim support programs.

To stay safe and supported, consider contacting a **rape crisis center** (*Frauenberatungsstelle*) or **Weißer Ring**, which offers counseling, legal guidance, and emotional support. Avoid showering or changing clothes before a medical exam if you think you may report the crime, as this helps preserve evidence. Most importantly, know that support services are confidential, nonjudgmental, and available whether or not you choose to involve the police.

Consular Assistance

If you're a victim of a crime while in Germany, your embassy or consulate can offer several forms of assistance to help you navigate the situation.

They can help you report the crime to the local police and provide a list of English-speaking lawyers, doctors, or counselors. They can assist in replacing a stolen passport, help you contact family or friends, and offer emotional support or referrals to local crisis services.

While they cannot investigate crimes, act as law enforcement, or pay for legal or medical costs, they can monitor your case, communicate with local authorities to ensure your rights are respected, and help you understand the legal process. They may also help with arranging emergency travel documents, provide information about local victim support services, and in some cases, assist with finding temporary shelter or emergency financial help through referral channels. Their role is to support your safety, well-being, and fair treatment while respecting German law.

 **General Questions**

1. *If I am a victim of a crime, can I legally be compensated as a non-citizen?* **Yes.** As a non-citizen, you can legally be compensated if you're a victim of a crime in Germany. Under the **Crime Victims Compensation Act**, foreign nationals—including tourists—may receive **financial support** for injuries or trauma from violent crimes that occur in Germany. This can include medical costs, therapy, and lost income. You'll need to report the crime and apply through the Federal Office of Justice. Your immigration status and cooperation may affect eligibility, but help is available through victim support services.

2. *If a family member falls victim to homicide, can I bring the body back to my home country?* **Yes.** If a family member is a victim of homicide in Germany, you can arrange to **repatriate the body** to your home country. This involves working with a local funeral home and your embassy or consulate, who can assist with documentation and refer you to reliable providers. You'll need a death certificate, coroner's report, and possibly official permission if an investigation is ongoing. While the family typically covers the cost, travel insurance may help. The embassy won't cover expenses but can guide and support you through the process.

3. *Are there any special considerations or rights for tourists who become victims of crimes in Germany?* Tourists who become victims of crimes in Germany are entitled to the **same legal protections as residents**. They can access victim assistance services for emotional, legal, and practical support. Tourists can report crimes in any language, and interpretation services are provided if needed. While tourists may not always qualify for the same compensation programs as residents, they can still be eligible for financial compensation for violent crimes through the Crime Victims Compensation Act. Tourists can also seek help from their embassy or consulate, which offers guidance on legal processes, emergency documents, and repatriation if necessary.

 **Safety Tips**

- If you are the victim of a crime, move to a safe location and dial **110 for police** or **112 for medical emergencies.** It's crucial to have these numbers easily accessible.

- **Be alert for tourist scams.** Stay vigilant in crowded areas like stations and markets. Common scams include pickpocketing through distraction tactics such as the "bump" or "bird poop" tricks. Be wary of overly friendly strangers.

- If sexually assaulted, find a safe place, avoid washing or changing clothes to preserve evidence, and call **110** to report the assault. You can request a translator or female officer for assistance.

- Embassies can help report the crime, replace stolen documents, and offer local legal and medical contacts. However, they cannot conduct investigations or pay legal costs.

- Record times, locations, suspect descriptions, and any available evidence like photos or receipts. This information can support police reports, insurance claims, and applications for crime victim compensation.

CHAPTER 15

POLICE

POLICE

Overview

The German police force is split into three main levels: **state police**, **federal police**, and **municipal (local) police**, each with its own responsibilities. Most of the everyday police work—like patrolling neighborhoods, handling crimes, and managing traffic—is done by the **state police**. Every one of Germany's 16 states has its own police force, and they handle things locally, just like in a big city police department.

The **federal police** work across the whole country. They don't deal with regular street crime, but instead focus on things like protecting borders, airports, and train stations. They also help the state police when needed, especially during big events or national emergencies. Some towns and cities have their own **local or municipal police**, but they usually just handle small things like parking violations or local rules—not serious crime. There's also a special federal agency called the **BKA** (akin to Germany's FBI), which steps in for crucial investigations like terrorism, cybercrime, or crimes that cross state or country borders.

In terms of personnel, Germany's police forces include over 330,000 employees. Of which, approximately 266,000 are sworn officers across both the state and federal levels. The majority—about 225,000—serve in the state police forces, while the Bundespolizei employs around

50,000 officers, and the BKA adds another 7,000 or so.[38] While the total number of officers is substantial, many state police forces report being **understaffed**, leading to high workloads and increased pressure on officers.

Police Response

In Germany, the police have a wide range of responsibilities aimed at ensuring public safety and upholding the law. Their key functions include **crime prevention and investigation, maintaining public order, responding to emergencies**, and **regulating traffic**. Crime investigation is typically handled by specialized branches like the *Kriminalpolizei*, while public order duties, especially during demonstrations or large events, often fall under the *Bereitschaftspolizei* (riot police) or even special tactical units like the SEK in high-risk situations. The *Bundespolizei* (Federal Police) play a significant role in securing the country's borders, railway stations, and airports. Additionally, the *Bundeskriminalamt* (BKA), Germany's federal criminal office, is tasked with tackling terrorism, cybercrime, and organized crime, and acts as the main liaison with international agencies.

Despite Germany's reputation for effective law enforcement, the police face several challenges. One of the most pressing issues is the **shortage of personnel**, particularly within the state police forces. Many officers are nearing retirement, and recruitment struggles to keep pace with demand. Alongside staffing issues, the rapid rise in cybercrime has highlighted deficiencies in digital infrastructure and training. The German police are also grappling with **public concerns over racial profiling** and the use of force, leading to scrutiny over how police interact with minority communities. Furthermore, there have been troubling reports of right-wing extremism among individual officers, prompting calls for stronger internal oversight and vetting.

---

38 https://www.destatis.de/EN/Themes/Government/Public-Service/Tables/
public-service-personnel-staff-police

However, efforts are underway to address this. Many states have increased the number of police academy slots, raised salaries, and offered more flexible working conditions. At the federal level, the Bundespolizei (Federal Police) has grown in recent years, in part due to increased duties related to border control, terrorism, and migration issues. Furthermore, the use of body cameras is being expanded across states to increase transparency and accountability. Many states have introduced enhanced training programs focusing on de-escalation techniques, anti-discrimination practices, and intercultural awareness.

Police and Community Relations

The overall public perception of the police in Germany is generally **positive**, though it varies depending on region, community, and recent events. Most Germans see the police as professional, reliable, and trustworthy, especially when it comes to everyday safety, traffic control, and emergency response. Surveys often show that a majority of the population trusts the police and believes they do a good job maintaining public order.

However, there are also **growing concerns and criticisms**, particularly among minority communities, younger people, and activists. Issues like **racial profiling, excessive use of force**, and **inadequate accountability mechanisms** have sparked public debates and protests in recent years. Cases involving police violence or right-wing extremism within police ranks have damaged trust in some parts of society, especially when investigations appear slow or lack transparency.

Efforts are being made to improve police-community relations, such as expanding the use of body cameras, improving diversity and cultural training, and increasing dialogue with local communities. While the foundation of trust is strong, there's a clear need for continued reforms to ensure that all groups in society feel equally protected and treated fairly by the police.

Police Use of Force

The police use of force is a **recognized issue in Germany**, though it's not considered as widespread or systemic as in some other countries. Nevertheless, studies suggest that while approximately 2,000 cases of police violence are officially recorded annually, the actual number may be much higher, potentially up to five times greater, indicating a substantial underreporting problem.[39]

Public concern has grown in recent years, particularly regarding how force is applied in specific contexts, such as protests, encounters with marginalized groups, and situations involving mental health crises. While the majority of police operations are carried out professionally, critics argue that there is insufficient transparency and accountability when incidents involving excessive force occur. Many cases are either underreported or not thoroughly investigated, leading to a perception that police are rarely held accountable for misconduct. This has led to calls for better oversight, independent review bodies, and increased use of body cameras to document police interactions. At the same time, there is ongoing debate about the balance between officer safety and citizens' rights, especially in high-pressure situations. As a result, police use of force remains a sensitive and important issue in public discourse and reform efforts.

 **Law of the Land True Story**

The forced eviction of climate activists from the German village of Lützerath in January 2023 reignited national debate over police use of force and the government's environmental policies. Lützerath, slated for demolition to expand the Garzweiler coal mine, had become a symbolic battleground for climate activists, who occupied the site in protest against what they view as climate hypocrisy. Although the

---

39 https://www.aa.com.tr/en/europe/
police-violence-in-germany-serious-underreported-problem

police claimed to prioritize de-escalation and allow peaceful exits, some protesters reported undue force during removals, with videos showing officers dragging demonstrators and using physical restraint.

Critics also pointed to the overwhelming police presence, including riot gear and water cannons, as unnecessarily aggressive. While the government and energy company RWE argue the mine's expansion is vital for energy security, activists dispute this, citing studies that show alternative energy strategies are viable. The episode exposed ongoing tensions between state authority and civil disobedience, with the response to the protest raising broader concerns about proportionality, freedom of expression, and the role of law enforcement in handling non-violent resistance.

HOW TO GET LEGAL HELP IN GERMANY

HOW TO GET LEGAL HELP IN GERMANY

Available Resources

If you find yourself needing legal help in Germany, there are several avenues you can pursue. Foreign nationals have the right to **contact their embassy or consulate** if they encounter legal trouble. Consular officials can provide a list of local attorneys, assist with translations or interpreters, and notify your family or legal representatives if needed. These services are especially important in cases of arrest or detention.

If you are arrested in Germany and you cannot afford legal representation, you may be assigned a **public defender** (*Pflichtverteidiger*), provided your case qualifies due to its seriousness. If you can afford one, it is always advisable to find a reliable lawyer. To find a qualified English-speaking lawyer in Germany, you can start by using the **Official Register of Lawyers** (*Bravsearch*). This online search tool allows you to filter by language, specialization, and location. Alternatively, websites like GermanPedia.com and aiel.com offer directories of English-speaking lawyers in Germany, often with client reviews and contact information.

 Your consulate is another good resource, as they often maintain lists of local attorneys that speak your language and are familiar with assisting foreign clients. Some travelers or expats also have legal insurance

(*Rechtsschutzversicherung*), and these providers can recommend or assign a lawyer on your behalf. **https://allaboutberlin.com/guides/legal-insurance**

Legal Aid[40]

Foreign visitors in Germany are eligible for legal aid under certain conditions. Legal aid is not limited to German citizens or residents; it is **based primarily on the applicant's financial situation and the merits of the case.** If you are a tourist or temporary visitor and you're involved in a legal matter in Germany, you can apply for legal assistance like a local resident would.

There are two main types of legal aid in Germany: *Beratungshilfe*, which covers the cost of legal advice outside of court, and *Prozesskostenhilfe*, which helps cover legal expenses during court proceedings. For *Beratungshilfe*, you need to apply at the local district court, *Amtsgericht*, usually before meeting with a lawyer, although a lawyer can also help you submit the request afterward. For *Prozesskostenhilfe*, the application is made as part of the court proceedings, and you must include detailed information about your income, assets, and living expenses. Supporting documents such as bank statements or proof of income will be required, and the court will decide based on your financial need and the likelihood of your case succeeding.

To qualify for legal aid, you must demonstrate that you cannot reasonably afford legal costs, that your case has a reasonable chance of success, and that the matter is not considered frivolous. In criminal cases, legal aid can come in the form of a **court-appointed defense lawyer**, called a *Pflichtverteidiger*. This is typically granted if the charges are serious, such as those carrying a sentence of over one year, or if the case is too complex for you to represent yourself effectively.

---

40 https://handbookgermany.de/en/legal-aid

Legal aid in Germany can cover a range of services. It may pay for initial consultations with a lawyer, court costs, and attorney fees throughout the trial. In some cases, it also includes the costs of interpreters or expert witnesses if necessary. If your financial situation improves within four years of receiving legal aid, the court may require partial or full repayment in installments.

If you're unsure where to begin, visiting the local district court or contacting a local lawyer is a good first step. Your country's embassy or consulate in Germany can also help guide you to legal resources.

Foreign Embassies in Germany

Foreign embassies and consulates in Germany play a vital role in supporting their citizens while they are abroad. Generally, embassies and consulates provide a **range of services**, including **assistance in legal or medical emergencies**, **help with lost or stolen passports**, **notarial services**, **support during arrests or detentions**, and **communication with family back home.** They also serve as a point of contact for their country's citizens during crises, such as natural disasters or political unrest, and often maintain lists of local attorneys, doctors, and interpreters. Additionally, they are responsible for **handling visa and immigration matters** for naturalized citizens wishing to travel to or work in their home country.

In Germany, foreign embassies are **primarily located in Berlin**, which is the capital and the seat of most diplomatic missions. In addition to Berlin, many countries have consulates in major cities like **Frankfurt**, **Munich**, **Hamburg**, **Düsseldorf**, and **Stuttgart**. These consulates handle regional matters and often provide more accessible services for people living outside of Berlin.

For U.S. citizens in Germany, the most prominent diplomatic missions include the U.S. Embassy in Berlin and consulates in Frankfurt and Munich. **The U.S. Embassy in Berlin** is the **main hub for diplomatic relations and political matters**, while the **Consulate General in Frankfurt** is **one of the largest U.S. consular operations in the** world and handles most visa and immigration services. **The Consulate General in Munich** focuses on Southern Germany and **provides consular services to U.S. citizens in the region.**

 To find embassy or consulate information for other countries in Germany, you can visit **embassies.net/ germany**, a directory that links to the websites of embassies and consulates from around the world. There, you can search by country to find the diplomatic missions operating in Germany, including their contact information, locations, and services offered.

MEDICAL FACILITIES & HOSPITALS

MEDICAL FACILITIES & HOSPITALS

Overview[41]

Germany's healthcare system is widely regarded as **one of the best in the world**. It's built on the principle of solidarity, meaning that everyone—regardless of income—has access to the same high standard of care. This approach ensures that healthcare in Germany is not only effective but also equitable. Like many other European countries, Germany has a **dual healthcare model** made up of both **public** and **private** systems. Participation in the healthcare system is **mandatory**, and both forms of insurance are available to anyone living in the country.

The healthcare system operates through a **shared contribution model**, where both employees and employers contribute to health insurance costs. **Public healthcare** is the most commonly used system and **provides comprehensive coverage** for the majority of the population. **Private healthcare**, while more expensive, is **an option for those with higher incomes**, self-employed individuals, or people with specific medical needs. It often includes faster access to specialists and more personalized care, making it a good option for those who require more intensive treatment or have ongoing conditions.

Everyone enrolled in German healthcare receives a **medical insurance card**, which gives them access to a wide range of services. This includes

---

41 https://germanpedia.com/german-healthcare-system/

doctor visits, hospital care, emergency treatment, and standard medical procedures. **Public healthcare covers most of the essential medical needs. Private healthcare**, on the other hand, **tends to cover services that are either partially or not covered by the public system**, such as certain dental treatments, advanced procedures, or alternative medicine.

In terms of quality, Germany's healthcare system is known for its **modern infrastructure, well-trained medical staff**, and **efficient treatment processes.** Patients are generally treated fairly and promptly. Private healthcare offers more flexibility and often shorter waiting times, but public care is still considered to be of an excellent standard.

Healthcare in Germany is **not free**, but it is structured to be **affordable.** On average, an adult might pay around US$450 a month for public insurance. While this may sound high, it's in line with average incomes and includes a broad range of healthcare services. For most people, this system offers a good balance between cost and coverage, especially considering the overall quality of care.

For non-emergency medical situations, patients typically contact their **general practitioner** (*Hausarzt*), who serves as the first point of contact and refers them to specialists when needed. Many clinics also offer after-hours services for urgent but non-life-threatening issues.

Some important numbers to keep in mind while traveling to Germany include:

- **112:** Fire department, ambulance, and general emergency services.
- **110:** Police.
- **116 117:** Non-emergency medical advice, staffed 24/7 by medical professionals, available when you need medical advice but it's not a life-threatening situation. You can call this number when you cannot reach your doctor's office or have questions about a virus.
- **19222:** In some regions, this number is used for non-emergency medical assistance and ambulance requests.
- **116 116:** Central card cancellation for reporting lost or stolen ID or passports and canceling credit cards.

Visitors' Access to Healthcare in Germany[42]

Visitors to Germany can access medical services quite easily, though the way they pay for care depends on their insurance coverage. Most short-term visitors, like tourists or business travelers, typically rely on **travel health insurance** purchased in their home country before arrival. This insurance often covers emergency care, doctor visits, and sometimes repatriation if needed. Some travelers from countries with reciprocal agreements with Germany (like those in the EU or EEA) can use their **European Health Insurance Card** (EHIC) to access public healthcare services at the same rates as German citizens. For everyone else, including travelers from the U.S., Canada, or Australia, any medical care must usually be paid for **out-of-pocket** or claimed back later through their insurance provider.

In Germany, out-of-pocket costs for visitors are relatively manageable compared to countries like the U.S., though the amount can vary depending on the treatment. The average costs for medical services in Germany include a consultation ranging from €30 - 60 (**US$32 - 65**), treatment around €100 (**US$110**), analysis and tests between €20 - 100 (**US$21-110**), and a medicine prescription costing €20 - 30 (**US$21 - 32**).[43]

Language barriers can sometimes present challenges, especially in smaller towns or rural areas where English is less commonly spoken. However, in larger cities and hospitals, many medical professionals speak at least basic English, and international patients are not unusual. Some hospitals even have international departments or staff trained to assist non-German-speaking patients. Pharmacies (Apotheken) also often have staff who speak English, and most medications are labeled with clear instructions. Still, it can be helpful to carry a translation app or a printed card with key medical terms if you don't speak German.

If you're traveling in Germany and need non-emergency care, it's best to visit a **general practitioner** or a **local clinic.** In urgent situations, dialing

---

42 https://www.air-dr.com/media/health/
     travelers-guide-to-healthcare-in-germany/#cost

43 https://expatrist.com/what-is-the-cost-of-medical-treatment-in-germany/

112 will connect you to emergency services. If you're unsure where to go, your hotel, embassy, or travel insurer can usually help direct you to the nearest English-speaking provider.

German Hospitals[44]

Germany has one of the most advanced and well-organized hospital systems in the world. The country is home to approximately **1,900 hospitals**, which include both public and private institutions. These hospitals are staffed by over **800,000 medical professionals**, including doctors, nurses, and specialists, reflecting Germany's strong focus on accessible, high-quality medical care.

Germany's hospitals are generally well-equipped and staffed compared to many countries, but in recent years there have been increasing concerns about **staff shortages**, particularly among nurses and support staff. While the country has a high standard of medical training and an extensive network of healthcare facilities, maintaining adequate staffing levels has become a growing challenge. In urban university hospitals and large private clinics, staffing is usually solid, and patients typically receive excellent care. However, in rural areas or smaller regional hospitals, understaffing can lead to longer wait times, heavier workloads for medical staff, and sometimes delays in non-emergency procedures.

Hospitals are spread throughout the country, but they are particularly concentrated in **major cities and metropolitan areas** such as **Berlin, Munich, Frankfurt, Hamburg**, and **Düsseldorf**. These urban centers host many of Germany's largest university hospitals and specialized clinics, offering cutting-edge treatments and attracting both domestic and international patients. Rural areas also have good hospital coverage, though highly specialized treatments may require travel to a larger city.

---

44 https://www.ceicdata.com/en/germany/health-care-statistics/ no-of-hospitals

Some of the **best-known hospitals** in Germany—recognized for their medical expertise, technology, and international patient services—include:

- **Charité – Universitätsmedizin Berlin:** One of Europe's largest university hospitals, highly respected in research and patient care across all fields of medicine.

- **University Hospital Heidelberg:** Known for excellence in cancer treatment, neurology, and transplant services.

- **University Hospital of Munich (LMU Klinikum):** Offers state-of-the-art care in a wide range of specialties and frequently ranks among the top hospitals in the country.

- **University Hospital Freiburg:** Well-known for its cardiac care, oncology, and neuroscience departments.

For **international visitors**, many hospitals in larger cities have **international departments** that offer multilingual support, coordination of care, and help with insurance matters. These departments are often set up to handle the needs of medical tourists, expats, or foreign patients seeking second opinions or specialized treatments. Hospitals like **Charité** in Berlin, **Schön Klinik** in Munich, and **Asklepios** hospitals in Hamburg are particularly experienced in this area. Not only do they accommodate language needs but also often have streamlined processes for international patients seeking treatment.

 **General Questions**

1. *What should you do if you feel unwell/sick in Germany?* If you feel unwell in Germany, what you do depends on how serious your symptoms are. For **mild issues** like a cold or stomach bug, visit a **general practitioner** (*Hausarzt*). You can find one nearby through your hotel, a pharmacy (*Apotheke*), or online. No referral is needed. If it's **outside regular hours**, call **116 117** to reach an on-call doctor or after-hours medical service.

   For **serious symptoms** like chest pain, difficulty breathing, or severe injury, go to the nearest hospital's **emergency room** (*Notaufnahme*). In a life-threatening situation, call **112** for an ambulance.

   Visitors should carry their **passport and travel insurance** information when seeking care. Most clinics and hospitals—especially in cities—have **English-speaking staff** and are used to treating international patients.

2. *What should I do if I need a prescription while in Germany?* If you need a prescription while in Germany, you should first visit a **general practitioner** (*Hausarzt*) or a specialist who can assess your condition. If needed, they will issue a prescription for medication. You can take this prescription to any **pharmacy** (*Apotheke*) to have it filled. Pharmacies are widespread, and most staff in larger cities can speak some English.

   If you're a visitor, make sure to bring your **travel insurance** information, as some insurance plans may cover the cost of prescribed medications. If you don't have insurance, you'll need to pay for the prescription out of pocket, but costs are usually reasonable compared to other countries.

   In case of an emergency or if you're unsure where to find a doctor, you can call **116 117** for non-emergency medical services or visit a hospital's emergency department.

Insurance Guidance

Foreign insurance plans in Germany are **generally accepted**, but the process depends on the type of insurance you have. Visitors with travel health insurance can usually be reimbursed for medical costs, but you might need to pay upfront and submit claims later. If you're from the EU and have an **EHIC** (**European Health Insurance Card**), you can access public healthcare at the same rates as German residents. For other international visitors, it's advisable to have **travel insurance** that specifically covers healthcare in Germany, as not all foreign plans are directly accepted by German hospitals and doctors.

The **average costs for medical services** in Germany can vary depending on the type of care. A **doctor's visit** typically costs between **€30 - 100** (**about US$32 - 107**), depending on the doctor and whether the visit is basic or requires more extensive consultation. **Emergency room visits** start around **€150** (**about US$160**) for initial care, and costs can rise if additional tests or treatments are needed.[45]

For payments, most medical providers in Germany expect payment upfront if you're not covered by German insurance. Visitors will need to pay by **credit card**, **debit card**, or **cash**. If you have travel insurance, you can keep your receipts and submit them for reimbursement after your treatment. In case of emergency, the hospital will usually expect payment upon discharge unless your insurance covers it directly.

It's always best to confirm with your travel insurance provider how reimbursement will work or whether direct billing is possible in your case.

---

45 https://expatrist.com/what-is-the-cost-of-medical-treatment-in-germany/

DRIVING IN GERMANY

DRIVING IN GERMANY

Overview[46]

Driving in Germany is generally a very positive experience, especially for those who enjoy **a well-organized and efficient road system**. The country is famous for its **Autobahn**, where large stretches have no general speed limit. German drivers tend to be disciplined and follow the rules closely, which helps maintain safety and predictability on the roads.

The condition of the **road infrastructure is excellent**. Highways (Autobahns) are typically in top shape, with regular maintenance and clear signage. Major routes like *Bundesstraßen* and rural roads (*Landstraßen*) are also very well-kept. City roads vary more but are usually reliable. You'll find signage to be standardized and easy to understand, especially if you're familiar with international road signs.

If you're driving as a visitor, you'll need a **valid driver's license**. Licenses from **EU or EEA countries** are fully accepted **without restrictions**. If you're from a **non-EU country**, you can drive for **up to six months using your home license**, although it's best to carry an **International Driving Permit** if your license isn't in English or German.

---

46 https://www.expatica.com/de/living/transportation/
driving-and-parking-in-germany-100916/?utm_source

For **insurance**, third-party liability is mandatory. If you're using a rental car, it will include the required coverage. If you're driving your own car from abroad, be sure to have **international insurance** that's valid in Germany—commonly referred to as a "**green card.**"

There are a few **unique customs and rules** that foreign drivers should be aware of. On the Autobahn, you must always use the **left lane only for overtaking** and return to the right as soon as you're done. Drivers expect this and will often flash their headlights if you're lingering in the passing lane. Merging onto the Autobahn is done quickly and assertively; hesitation can be dangerous. The "**zipper merge**" rule (called *Reißverschlussverfahren*) is strictly observed when two lanes merge. Drivers are expected to take turns. Also, unlike in some countries, turning right at a red light is not allowed unless a small green arrow sign is present. **Roundabouts** are common, and vehicles inside the roundabout always have the right of way.

In terms of tolls, **Germany does not charge private passenger cars to use the Autobahn**. Tolls mainly apply to heavy goods vehicles. However, if you're traveling through neighboring countries like Austria or Switzerland, you'll often need a prepaid toll sticker (called a **vignette**), so it's important to check if your route crosses borders. Within Germany, some tunnels or mountain roads may charge fees, but this is rare for everyday routes. When tolls are present, payment is usually possible by credit or debit card, and cash is accepted at staffed booths. Some systems also use electronic tolling for trucks.

 ## Main Traffic Rules & Road Safety Tips

- **Driving side:** Right side of the road.

- **Speed limits:**

  - **Built-up areas:** 50 km/h (31 mph).

  - **Outside built-up areas:** 90 km/h (55 mph) to 100 km/h (62 mph)

- **City roads:** 30 km/h (18 mph)
- **Motorways:** 130 km/h (80 mph); vehicles must be able to reach a minimum speed of 60 km/h (37 mph)

- **Traffic signals:** Red (top), yellow (middle), green (bottom) system. The yellow light flashes twice to give drivers more warning.

- **Seat belts:** Seat belts are required by all persons in the vehicle at all times.

- **Mobile devices:** Using a mobile phone while driving is illegal unless hands-free.

- **Alcohol:** The legal **BAC limit is 0.05 percent** for most drivers, but a strict **0.00 percent** applies to those **under 21, new drivers,** and **commercial drivers.** Even small amounts of alcohol can lead to penalties if driving impaired.

- **Toll roads:** Generally free for private passenger cars, but applicable to trucks and commercial vehicles over 7.5 tons. Always check route-specific toll requirements before your journey.

- **If stopped by police:** Remain calm and follow the instructions. Police officers may ask for your driver's license, vehicle registration, and proof of insurance. It's standard to stay inside your vehicle unless instructed otherwise. Most officers speak some English, especially on major routes.

- **Road safety tips:**

  - Be aware of speed limits
  - Understand priority rules at intersections and roundabouts
  - Always carry the necessary documents and equipment
  - Follow driving rules, road signs, and traffic lights
  - Observe parking rules

General Questions

1. *Can I use my driver's license from my home country to drive in Germany?* **Yes.** You can use your driver's license from your home country in Germany for **up to six months** if you're a visitor. If your license is not in German or English, it's recommended to carry an International Driving Permit (IDP) as a translation. EU/EEA licenses are valid without restriction. If you plan to stay longer than six months, you may need to exchange your license depending on your country of origin.

2. *What is the age requirement for renting a car in Germany?* The minimum age to rent a car in Germany is typically **18 years old**, but this can vary depending on the rental company and the type of vehicle. Many rental agencies set their minimum age at **21**, and some may require drivers to be **25** for certain vehicles, especially luxury or high-performance models.

Law of the Land Hypothetical

HYPOTHETICAL: *Jason, a tourist from the United States, is driving through Germany with his friend. They rented a car in Berlin and are planning to visit several cities across the country. While driving through Cologne, Jason notices a sign that says "Umweltzone" (environmental zone) but assumes it doesn't apply to tourists. Later, he's pulled over by police and fined €80 (about $ 91 USD). Was Jason legally required to have an emissions sticker, even though he was driving a rental car as a visitor?*

ANSWER: *Yes. Jason needed a valid **Umweltplakette** (emissions sticker) to drive in a designated **Umweltzone** (low-emission zone), which are found in many German cities. All vehicles, including rentals, must display this sticker to enter these areas. However, this **rule doesn't apply to highways (Autobahns)**. It's the driver's responsibility to ensure* *the car has the sticker, even if it's a rental. It is always a good idea to check if your route goes through an Umweltzone.*

NUDE BEACHES & CLOTHING-OPTIONAL RESORTS

NUDE BEACHES & CLOTHING-OPTIONAL RESORTS

Overview

Nudism—referred to as **Freikörperkultur (FKK)** or "free body culture"—is culturally accepted in Germany and has a long tradition. It's seen as a natural and non-sexual expression of freedom and body positivity, especially in former East Germany, where it became particularly popular during the 20th century.

Germany boasts a number of nudist-friendly hotels, resorts, and campgrounds, dedicated to naturism and regular accommodations with clothing-optional facilities. Most are located in rural or seaside areas, and they follow clear etiquette rules where respect for personal space and non-sexual behavior is strictly expected.

Legality and Safety[47]

There are no explicit national laws that outright prohibit or permit public nudity in Germany and nudism is well-regulated through designated areas known as **FKK (Freikörperkultur) zones**. These include specific beaches, parks, lakesides, saunas, and campgrounds where public nudity

---

47 https://sandee.com/blog/nudism-laws-in-germany

is officially permitted. Nudity on private grounds is legal even if visible from outside. However, appearing nude outside these designated areas may be considered a minor legal offense if it causes public disturbance or offense, potentially leading to fines if complaints are made. Local authorities have the discretion to enforce regulations related to nudity, especially in public spaces where social norms differ. In practice, enforcement is relatively relaxed, especially in areas where nudism has a cultural tradition, but it's still important to follow local guidelines.

Safety in nudist areas is maintained through enforcement of local regulations and social norms. For example, in Rostock, beach wardens have the power to ban visitors wearing clothing on nudist-only beaches to protect the comfort and rights of naturists. These regulations are designed to prevent conflicts and ensure that the spaces remain welcoming for those practicing naturism.

Authorities respond primarily to complaints that arise due to inappropriate behavior, and enforcement tends to focus on disruptive actions rather than nudity itself.

Adhering to established **etiquette** is essential for a respectful and enjoyable nudist experience in Germany. Maintaining personal space is important to ensure others' privacy without making them feel uncomfortable. Photography is strictly prohibited without clear consent, and staring or making unsolicited comments about others' bodies is considered highly inappropriate. Any sexual behavior or conduct perceived as offensive is not tolerated and may lead to legal consequences. Cleanliness is expected; visitors should dispose of trash properly and treat the natural surroundings with care. Avoid inappropriate behavior and be respectful of others' privacy. By following the established etiquette, individuals can enjoy a safe and positive experience while embracing the values of freedom, body acceptance, and connection with nature.

? General Questions

1. *Are there specific beaches in Germany that are well-known for nudism?* **Yes**. Germany is home to several well-known beaches where nudism is both common and accepted. Some popular nudist beaches in Germany include:

> **Sylt Island**: Located in the North Sea, Sylt is one of Germany's most famous destinations for naturists, featuring several FKK beaches, with wide stretches of sand where nudists can relax and enjoy the scenery. Sylt is well known for its laid-back atmosphere and is a popular destination for both locals and international visitors.

> **Usedom Island**: Situated on the Baltic Sea, the island has many beaches where nudism is openly practiced. Its long, sandy beaches are perfect for those looking to experience nudism in a peaceful and natural setting. The island also offers a mix of modern amenities and tranquil nature, making it a great spot for both relaxation and exploration.

> **Norderney Island**: Another island in the North Sea, Norderney offers a combination of beauty and history with several designated nudist beaches. These beaches are equipped with facilities and are part of Germany's larger tradition of seaside naturism.

> **FKK Beach at Langeoog**: Located in the East Frisian Islands, Langeoog is famous for its family-friendly naturist beaches. It's a more relaxed environment where both families and individuals can enjoy the freedom of being clothing-optional in a natural setting.

Strandbad Wannsee (Berlin): Located just outside Berlin, Strandbad Wannsee is one of the largest and most popular lakeside beaches for nudists. It offers a large FKK zone and is easily accessible from the city. It's a great spot for tourists looking to experience a naturist environment close to the capital.

2. *What are the rules and regulations regarding nudist saunas and spas in Germany, and how should travelers prepare for their visit?* In Germany, nudist saunas and spas are a key part of the wellness culture, and nudity is not only allowed but expected in most public sauna and spa areas. Travelers should be prepared to follow basic etiquette, such as showering thoroughly before entering and sitting on a towel in shared spaces for hygiene reasons. It's important to note that wearing swimsuits or clothing is generally prohibited, and maintaining a quiet, respectful atmosphere is essential. Many spas also have designated areas for men or women, and some may offer specific days or times for each gender. Flash photography or taking photos is usually prohibited to ensure privacy, and visitors should start slowly with the heat if they're new to sauna culture.

 ## Law of the Land Hypothetical

HYPOTHETICAL: *Sophia, a tourist from the UK, is staying at a naturist resort in Germany. After enjoying the nudist areas, she decides to explore the resort and enters a new section where some people are still wearing clothes. Did Sophia break any rules by being fully nude in a clothing-optional area, and what should she have known before entering?*

ANSWER: **No.** *Sophia did not break any rules by being fully nude, but she should have been aware that the clothing-optional area did not require nudity. While nudity is generally encouraged in naturist resorts, areas designated as clothing-optional allow visitors to choose whether* *or not to be nude. In such zones, it's important for visitors to respect the local etiquette and adjust accordingly.*

UNUSUAL LAWS

UNUSUAL LAWS

Overview

Unusual laws can be fascinating glimpses into a culture's values and history. While most people are aware of common legal restrictions, it's often the strange and quirky laws that capture our attention. These regulations can range from the amusing to the absurd, reflecting the unique circumstances and traditions of a place. Whether they arise from historical events, societal norms, or simply peculiar local customs, unusual laws can provide insight into the quirks of human behavior and governance.

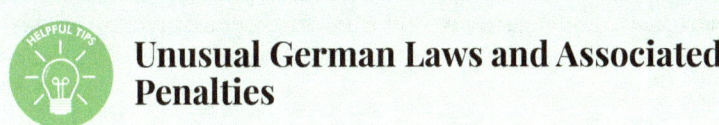

Unusual German Laws and Associated Penalties

Germany is known for its strict regulations, and some of its laws might seem unusual or quirky to visitors. Here are a few examples of unique laws, along with the penalties for breaking them:

Recycling Laws

Germany is a leader in recycling, and proper waste sorting is crucial. If you fail to recycle or dispose of your waste incorrectly, you could face

heavy fines. Local authorities are very strict about sorting recyclables properly, especially in residential areas.

Running Out of Fuel on the Autobahn

On the famous German Autobahn, stopping is strictly prohibited unless necessary for safety. If your vehicle runs out of fuel, it forces you to stop, and this could result in a **hefty fine** from law enforcement. The penalty is usually because stopping on the Autobahn can be dangerous for both you and other drivers.

Keeping Ashes at Home

In Germany, it's illegal to keep human ashes at home. The country considers human remains to be toxic, and as such, they must be stored in a proper facility. Failure to comply can lead to **legal consequences**, though the specific penalty may depend on the situation.

Offensive Language Toward Officials

In Germany, using curse words or calling an officer "stupid" during an interaction can lead to **heavy fines.** If the behavior is severe or continues, **arrest** is possible. The German authorities take respect for officials seriously, and aggressive or offensive behavior can quickly escalate.

Baby Name Restrictions

The German government has the right to reject unusual or non-sensical baby names. If a parent tries to name their child something deemed inappropriate, the government can intervene. While there's no direct financial penalty, parents may be forced to choose a different name, and the child's birth certificate may not be issued until the name is approved.

Quiet Sundays

Sunday in Germany is reserved for rest, and most shops are closed. In addition, it's illegal to do noisy activities, like home renovations or drilling, because it disturbs the peace. Violating this rule could lead to fines, and neighbors might complain about the disturbance.

 **General Questions**

1. *Is it illegal to flush the toilet after 10 p.m. in some apartment buildings in Germany, and what are the penalties for doing so?* **Yes.** In some apartment buildings in Germany, especially in older or more densely populated areas, it's considered **illegal to flush the toilet after 10 PM** due to **noise pollution** concerns. This rule is part of the country's **"quiet hours"** (*Ruhezeiten*), which generally run from 10 p.m. to 6 a.m. The idea is to avoid disturbing neighbors, particularly in apartment complexes where noise can carry easily. The penalty for violating this could be a **warning** or a **fine**, depending on how strict the building's regulations are. If you're in an apartment, it's always best to be mindful of these quiet hours.

2. *Is it illegal to play loud music in your car in Germany, and what are the potential consequences for doing so?* **Yes.** It is **illegal to play loud music in your car** in Germany, especially if it disturbs the peace. Under **German noise regulations**, there are laws that prohibit loud noise in public spaces, including music played in vehicles. This is particularly enforced in residential areas, at night, or in traffic. If you're caught playing excessively loud music, you could face a fine. The fine can vary depending on the situation, but generally, fines for disturbing the peace can range from **€20 - 100** (approximately **US$22 - 110**). Repeated offenses may also result in **warnings** or more severe penalties, including potential suspension of your driving license. It's important to be mindful of the volume, especially in residential areas or during quiet hours (usually from 10 PM to 6 AM).

TRAVELING SAFELY

TRAVELING SAFELY

Ladies Traveling Solo

Germany is considered **one of the safest countries in Europe**, known for its efficient law enforcement and strict regulations. It is generally regarded as a **safe** country for both locals and tourists, with **low crime rates** in most areas. Same holds true for **solo female travelers**.

Many women travel alone throughout the country without encountering any major issues. Public transportation is reliable, and major cities like Berlin, Munich, and Hamburg have good infrastructure, with well-lit streets and a high level of general safety. However, as with any country, it's important to stay aware of your surroundings, especially in unfamiliar or less busy areas at night.

In general, **areas to avoid** are the same as in any large country. In larger cities like Berlin, parts of **Neukölln** and **Kreuzberg**, and areas around **Frankfurt's main train station** (*Bahnhofsviertel*) can have higher rates of petty crime, such as pickpocketing. Similarly, districts like **St. Pauli** in Hamburg and some parts of **Duisburg** or **Essen** may not be as safe, particularly after dark. While these areas are generally not dangerous, it's always a good idea to stay vigilant, especially in busy public spaces or less well-lit areas at night.

Here are some general safety precautions to take as a female solo traveler:

- **Research your destination thoroughly:** Check current travel advisories and local news before visiting any area. Talk to the hotel or resort personnel or a trusted local about what areas to avoid.

- **Stick to well-populated areas:** Avoid venturing into isolated areas, especially at night.

- **Use licensed taxis and ride-sharing services:** Be cautious about using street taxis and always confirm the route with the driver.

- **Inform someone of your plans:** Let a trusted friend or family member know your itinerary and expected return times.

- **Be aware of your surroundings:** Stay vigilant and trust your instincts.

- **Dress modestly in certain areas:** Depending on the region, dressing conservatively can help you avoid unwanted attention.

- **Learn basic German phrases:** Knowing a few basic German phrases can be helpful for communication.

Traveling as a Family

Traveling with children in Germany is generally **very safe**, as the country is known for its high standards of healthcare, well-maintained infrastructure, and child-friendly environment. However, there are a few safety and health precautions to consider when traveling with kids.

First, ensure you have **adequate travel insurance** that covers medical expenses for the entire family. Germany has an excellent healthcare system, but medical treatments can be expensive without insurance. It's also important to familiarize yourself with emergency numbers, with **112** for medical emergencies and **110** for police emergencies.

When traveling by car, remember that children under 12 or under 150 cm (about 4'11") must be in a suitable child seat. Also, be cautious when crossing roads, as German drivers are known for their strict adherence to traffic rules. As for food and water safety, tap water is safe to drink in Germany, but if your child has a sensitive stomach, consider purchasing bottled water. When eating at restaurants, make sure food is freshly pre-pared to avoid any foodborne illnesses.

If your child has any medical conditions or allergies, be sure to carry all necessary medications. Germany's pharmacies are well-stocked, and most staff members speak some level of English, so you should have no trouble finding what you need if should you run out of something.

Germany offers plenty of child-friendly activities, such as amusement parks, zoos, museums with interactive exhibits, and outdoor activities like hiking and cycling. Planning your trip around these options will en-sure your children are entertained and engaged. Last, depending on the time of year, prepare for Germany's weather. Winters can be cold, so make sure children are bundled up; while summers can get warm, so sun protection and hydration are key.

By taking these simple health and safety precautions, traveling with chil-dren in Germany can be an enjoyable and worry-free experience.

Advice for All Travelers

Traveling in Germany is generally a smooth and enjoyable experience, but there are a few things to keep in mind to ensure your trip goes with-out a hitch. Germany has a strong culture of **punctuality**, so be mindful of being on time for appointments, public transportation, or any orga-nized tours. Public transport in cities is reliable and efficient, but make sure to always **validate your ticket** before getting on the train, tram, or bus, as there are hefty fines for traveling without one.

When it comes to **tipping**, it's customary but not obligatory. In restau-rants, it's polite to round up the bill or add a tip of about 5-10 percent. For taxis or other services, a tip of 1-2 euros (about $1.14 -2.28 USD) is appreciated.

Germany is a **cash-oriented society**, and while credit cards are increas-ingly accepted, it's a good idea to carry cash, especially in smaller towns or rural areas where card payments may not be as common. **ATMs** are widely available, and most major banks accept international cards, but always check if there are fees for withdrawing money abroad.

In terms of **personal safety**, Germany is generally very safe, but like any destination, it's important to stay vigilant, especially in crowded areas such as train stations or tourist hotspots where pickpocketing can occur. Be cautious with your belongings and avoid displaying expensive items or large amounts of cash.

Germany is known for its **strict laws**, so be aware of local customs and rules. For example, **noise regulations** are taken seriously, particularly on Sundays and public holidays, when most businesses are closed, and it's illegal to do anything that might disturb the peace (like loud music or home renovations). Be respectful of these cultural norms.

If you're planning to drive in Germany, the **Autobahn** is famous for its lack of speed limits in certain areas, but you should always drive cautiously, especially in busy or unknown regions. Also, make sure your vehicle complies with **traffic laws**, such as having a first-aid kit and reflective vest in the car, as these are required by law. Always adhere to the **zero-tolerance alcohol policy** for drivers under 21 years old, and be mindful of **pedestrian zones**, where vehicles are restricted.

 ## Do's and Don'ts While in Germany

When visiting Germany, there are several key customs and guidelines to keep in mind for a smooth and respectful experience:

- **Do** *be punctual*, as Germans value timeliness in all aspects of life, whether it's meetings, public transport, or appointments.

- **Don't** *make noise on Sundays*, as Germany has strict regulations about noise, and activities like home renovations or loud music are not permitted.

- **Do** *respect the environment* by recycling properly, as Germany's recycling system is one of the best in the world.

- **Don't** *tip excessively or too little*, as tipping in Germany is customary but should be moderate—around 5 - 10 percent in restaurants and a small tip for taxis or services.

- **Do** *greet people with a firm handshake* and use titles like Herr or Frau when addressing others in formal settings.

- **Don't** *discuss sensitive topics openly*, as Germans tend to be reserved about personal matters, and it's best to avoid controversial topics like politics, especially with strangers.

- **Do** *learn a few basic German phrases*, such as *"Guten Morgen"* (Good morning) or *"Danke"* (Thank you), to show appreciation for the culture.

- **Don't** *ignore pedestrian zones*, as many German cities have areas where vehicles are restricted. Be mindful and avoid driving in these zones.

- **Do** *bring a small gift* like flowers or wine a thoughtful gesture when invited to someone's home.

- **Don't** *overstay your welcome* and leave at appropriate time, as Germans typically value a sense of structure and routine, especially on weekdays.

TOURIST TAXATION

TOURIST TAXATION

Overview

Tourism plays a vital role in Germany's economy, contributing significantly to employment, foreign exchange earnings, and GDP growth. In 2023, this sector contributed close to €355 billion (US$404.47 billion) to the national economy, representing 9.3 percent of the economy and creating more than 168,000 jobs.[48] As one of the most popular travel destinations in Europe, tourism supports a wide range of industries, including hospitality, transportation, retail, and cultural activities. The sector is a major driver of economic development, particularly in areas like Bavaria, Berlin, and the Bavarian Alps, where tourism is integral to both urban and rural economies.

Tourists in Germany are required to pay taxes to help fund the public services and infrastructure that make the country an attractive place to visit. These taxes are often levied on accommodation and activities, and their purpose is to ensure that tourism contributes to maintaining and improving public services, such as transportation, waste management, and cultural institutions. By paying these taxes, tourists help sustain the tourism sector while benefiting from high-quality services during their stay.

---

48 https://wttc.org/news-article/wttc-predicts-germanys-travel-and-tourism-sector-to-rebound-to-95-percent-of-pre-pandemic-levels

Tourist Taxes in Germany[49]

Germany applies several forms of tourist-related taxes that are levied at the **municipal level**, so the rates and rules vary by city or region. The most common types are the **Kurtaxe (visitor's tax)**, the **Beherbergungssteuer (bed tax or lodging tax)**, and the **City or Culture Tax (Kulturförderabgabe)**.

The **Kurtaxe** is most commonly found in spa towns, health resorts, and scenic regions like the Bavarian Alps, the Black Forest, or Baltic Sea coast. It is a **fixed fee charged per adult, per night**, typically ranging from **€1 - 4 (approximately US$1.10 - 4.30)**, depending on the municipality. Children, students, and individuals with disabilities may be eligible for reduced rates or exemptions. Tourists paying this tax often receive a **guest card** (*Kurkarte*) that grants them benefits such as free public transportation, discounts at local attractions, or access to wellness facilities.

In larger cities, the **Beherbergungssteuer**, or lodging tax, is more common. This tax is usually a percentage of the net accommodation cost, most often **5% to 7.5 percent**, which translates into an additional **€5 – 11 (US$5.40 – 11.80)** on a hotel stay. It typically only applies to **leisure travelers**. Business travelers may be exempt but often need to provide documentation (such as a business letter or invoice) at the time of check-in or check-out to prove the nature of their stay.

The **City Tax or Culture Tax** (*Kulturförderabgabe*) is similar in purpose and is collected in several cities such as Berlin, Cologne, and Hamburg. Like the lodging tax, it's based on a percentage of the nightly room price, with rates varying but usually falling between **5 percent and 7 percent**. For example, a hotel stay costing €100 (about US$114) per night may include an added **€5 – 7 (US$5.40 – 7.50)** in city tax. The revenue goes toward funding **cultural services**, **city beautification**, **tourism promotion**, and the **upkeep of public spaces**.

---

49 https://www.german-way.com/the-rising-costs-for-tourists-in-germany/)

Whether you're staying in a hotel, hostel, or vacation rental, these taxes are **collected by the accommodation provider**. You'll typically pay them either during the booking process or at the check-in/check-out stage, with the tax amount itemized separately on your receipt or invoice.

Unlike many other countries, Germany **does not charge an exit or departure tax**. You can leave the country by plane, train, or car without paying any kind of border fee or departure surcharge. Airport taxes are included in your airline ticket price and are not considered separate tourist taxes. Likewise, Germany **does not have a general entry or arrival tax** for tourists.

Tourists in Germany do pay **VAT**, which is included in the price of most goods and services—**19 percent for standard items and percent% for some goods** like food and books. However, **non-EU tourists** can get a **VAT refund on goods** (not services) they export home, provided they spend at least €50 (about US$54) at one store, leave the EU within 90 days, and get their refund form stamped by customs upon departure. Hotel stays, meals, and services are **not eligible** for VAT refunds.[50]

 **Law of the Land Hypothetical**[51]

HYPOTHETICAL: *David, a tourist from the United States, spends €300 ($325 USD) on designer clothes in Berlin. The store staff gives him a VAT refund form and explains that he can get back part of the 19 percent VAT upon leaving the EU. However, when David arrives at the airport, he realizes he packed the items in his checked luggage and doesn't have them with him at customs. Can a tourist receive a VAT refund in Germany without showing the purchased items to customs before leaving the EU?*

50 https://www.germany.info/us-en/service/09-taxes/vat-refund-906296

51 https://wise.com/gb/blog/vat-refund-germany

ANSWER: *No. German customs law requires that the actual* **goods be presented**—*unopened and unused*—**alongside the VAT refund form and receipts** *at a designated customs desk* **before check-in**. *This step is crucial because customs must verify the items are leaving the EU. If David's purchases are already in checked luggage, he cannot present them for inspection, and his refund will be denied. To avoid this, travelers should always keep VAT-refund-eligible goods in their carry-on baggage until after the customs process.*

LONG-TERM STAYS

CHAPTER 23

LONG-TERM STAYS

Overview

People choose to stay long-term in Germany for a variety of reasons. One of the biggest draws is the **strong economy** and **stable job market**, especially in industries like engineering, IT, healthcare, and research. Germany is known for offering a **high quality of life**, with clean cities, efficient public transportation, low crime rates, and excellent infrastructure. Students often come for the **low or even free university tuition** and decide to stay because of the post-graduation job opportunities and supportive visa options. The **healthcare system** is another major advantage. It's well-funded, reliable, and accessible to all legal residents. And for many, Germany's central location in Europe, cultural richness, and historic charm are part of the appeal too. Whether you're into classical music, techno clubs, hiking, or history, there's something for everyone.

When it comes to the best cities or regions for long-term living, **Berlin** is often at the top. It's vibrant, diverse, and full of opportunity, especially for creatives and people in tech. **Munich** offers a more polished, clean-cut environment with lots of economic opportunities, though the cost of living there is among the highest in Germany. **Hamburg** has a mix of elegance and industry, with a strong expat presence and access to nature. **Frankfurt** is ideal for those in finance or international business, and it's incredibly well-connected by air. If you're looking for something more affordable or artistic, cities like **Leipzig** and **Dresden** have become magnets for students, creatives, and remote workers. Smaller towns like

Heidelberg and **Freiburg** offer a slower pace of life and are great for families and academics.

Living Costs in Germany

Germany offers a **moderate cost of living** compared to many Western countries, particularly when you factor in the quality of public services, healthcare, and infrastructure. While it's more expensive than many parts of Eastern Europe or Latin America, it's generally more affordable than countries like the U.S., the UK, or Switzerland.

Rent is one of the biggest monthly expenses. In cities like Berlin or Leipzig, a one-bedroom apartment typically costs between €800 – 1,200 (US$850 – 1,275) per month. In higher-cost cities like Munich or Frankfurt, similar apartments can range from €1,200 – 1,800 (US$1,275 – 1,915). Utilities are usually an additional €150 – 250 (US$160 – 265) monthly, depending on the size of the apartment and usage. A standard monthly "broadcasting fee" (*Rundfunkbeitrag*) of around €18 (US$19) also applies.

Groceries are quite affordable, especially when shopping at discount supermarkets like Aldi, Lidl, or Penny. Staples like bread, milk, and fresh produce are significantly cheaper than in the U.S., though imported goods can be pricier. Dining out is budget-friendly, with meals ranging from €4 – 6 (US$4.25 – 6.35) for casual street food to €10 – 20 (US$10.60 – 21.20) at mid-range restaurants.

Germany's public transportation system is both efficient and cost-effective. Most cities offer monthly transit passes from €49 – 100 (US$52 – 106), and the Deutschlandticket allows unlimited travel on regional trains and local transit throughout the country for €49 (US$52) per month. This makes it easy and economical to get around without a car.

Housing Options for Long-Term Stays

Long-term housing in Germany is centered around renting, which is the norm even among locals. The market offers everything from cozy downtown apartments in historic buildings to suburban homes and modern flats. Germany has **strong tenant protection laws**, and leases often last for years, offering renters a sense of stability and security.

Rental prices vary widely by location. In Berlin, you can find a one-bedroom apartment for about €900 – 1,200 (US$955 – 1,275) per month. In Munich, that same apartment might cost €1,500 – 1,800 (US$1,595 – 1,915). More affordable cities like Leipzig or Dresden offer similar rentals for around €700 – 1,000 (US$745 – 1,065). Many expats start in furnished rentals or shared apartments (WGs) while getting settled.

Buying property is also possible and common for long-term residents. There are **no legal restrictions for foreigners purchasing real estate** in Germany. However, you'll typically need a down payment of 20–30 percent, and property prices—especially in urban centers—can be high. Rural and suburban areas offer much more affordable options and a slower pace of life.

Healthcare Options Available for Long-Term Residents

Germany's healthcare system is highly regarded for its quality, accessibility, and structure. **Health insurance is mandatory for all legal long-term residents**, and there are two main systems to choose from: public (statutory) insurance and private insurance.

Public health insurance (*Gesetzliche Krankenversicherung*) is used by the majority of residents and is income-based. Contributions are around 14–15 percent of your gross salary, with employers covering half. For example, someone earning €3,000 (US$3,190) a month might pay around €210 – 225 (US$225 – 240) in monthly contributions. This includes doctor visits, hospital care, and prescriptions, with low out-of-pocket costs.

Private health insurance is available to freelancers, higher earners, or those opting out of the public system. It can offer shorter wait times and more flexible coverage but becomes more expensive with age or pre-existing conditions. Many doctors in urban areas speak English, and medical care is available across the country, even in smaller towns.

Transportation Options

Germany's transportation network is one of the best in the world. Cities have **extensive systems of buses, trams, subways (U-Bahn), and commuter trains (S-Bahn)**, and almost every region is connected by the Deutsche Bahn national rail service. The monthly Deutschlandticket, priced at €49 (US$52), offers unlimited travel on most forms of public transport throughout the country, making it ideal for residents.

In larger cities, many people don't own cars at all. Instead, they rely on public transit, bikes, or car-sharing apps like Share Now. **Taxis and ride-sharing services like Uber are available in most urban areas.** In rural regions, however, owning a car is often necessary due to limited public transit. Gasoline and car insurance can be pricey, but roads are well maintained, and the famous Autobahn network makes travel quick and efficient.

Germany is also **very bike-friendly**, with most cities offering designated bike lanes, bike parking, and even public bike-sharing systems. E-scooters have also become popular for short commutes or errands in urban areas.

Language Considerations

While **many Germans—especially younger people and professionals—speak English**, German is the official language and plays a big role in everyday life. Learning at least basic German is important for long-term residents, especially when it comes to dealing with bureaucracy, visiting doctors, or renting housing.

Language schools and integration courses are widely available and often subsidized or free for new residents. In cities like Berlin, Hamburg, and Frankfurt, it's possible to get by with English in many situations, but speaking German will help with forming relationships and navigating daily life more easily.

Even if you arrive with no German knowledge, it's common for expats to start learning after arrival through apps, classes, or immersion. Over time, learning the language greatly enhances your experience and sense of belonging.

Long-Term Visas[52]

If you're planning to stay in Germany for more than just a short visit, you'll need to look into one of the country's **long-term visa options**. Germany offers a wide range of residence permits designed for professionals, students, freelancers, researchers, and families. Each type of visa has its own set of requirements, but overall, the country provides a well-structured and relatively accessible pathway for people looking to live, work, or study there long-term. Whether you're moving for a job, pursuing a degree, or simply starting a new chapter of life, there's likely a visa route that fits your plans.

Here are the main long-term visa options available in Germany:

Work Visa / Employment Visa:

This visa is for non-EU nationals who have a job offer in Germany. To qualify, your job typically needs to match your qualifications, and the salary must meet a minimum threshold (which varies by profession).

If approved, you'll receive a residence permit tied to your employment contract, and it can be extended or lead to permanent residency after a few years.

EU Blue Card:

This is a special type of work visa aimed at highly skilled professionals, especially in fields like IT, engineering, healthcare, and academia. To qualify, you generally need:

- A university degree

---

52 https://www.germany-visa.org

- **A job offer with a minimum annual salary (as of 2024):** around €45,300 (US$48,200), or lower in shortage professions like tech or health)

The EU Blue Card offers faster paths to permanent residency and allows easier mobility within the EU.

Job Seeker Visa

This visa allows qualified professionals to enter Germany for **up to 6 months** to look for a job. You need a recognized university degree and proof you can support yourself financially during your stay. If you find a job during that time, you can switch to a work visa or EU Blue Card.

Freelancer/Self-Employment Visa

Germany welcomes freelancers, particularly in creative, tech, and media fields. This visa is common in cities like Berlin, where there's a strong freelance community. Requirements include:

- Proof of relevant work or clients in Germany
- A viable business or freelance plan
- Health insurance
- Enough savings or income to support yourself

For more traditional entrepreneurs (like opening a business or investing), there's a separate **Self-Employment Visa**, which requires a solid business plan and economic benefit to the local economy.

Student Visa

For those accepted into a German university or preparatory course, this visa allows you to stay for the duration of your studies and work part-time.

After graduation, you can apply for an **18-month job search visa** and then switch to a work visa once employed.

Language Course Visa

If you're coming specifically to learn German, you can apply for a language course visa that allows you to stay in Germany while enrolled in an intensive language course (usually **3–12 months**). It does not permit work and usually can't be converted into another visa type from within the country.

Family Reunification Visa

If your spouse, parent, or child lives legally in Germany (as a citizen or residence permit holder), you may be eligible to join them. Spouses may need to prove basic German language skills (A1 level), though exceptions exist. Once approved, you typically get a residence permit that may allow you to work.

Research Visa

For academic researchers or scientists who have an agreement with a research institution in Germany. This visa is part of the EU's effort to attract global talent in academia.

Residency for Retirement or "Non-Working" Stay (Limited Option)

Germany doesn't offer a retirement visa like some other countries (e.g., Portugal or Mexico), but in some cases, retirees can apply for a long-term residence permit if they can prove sufficient income, health insurance, and ties to Germany. These are usually granted on a case-by-case basis, and approval is not guaranteed.

Most long-term visas for Germany share a core set of requirements, regardless of whether you're applying for work, study, family reunification, or self-employment. First, you'll need a **valid passport with sufficient remaining validity**, along with a **completed national visa application**

form and **two recent biometric passport photos**. A key part of the process is demonstrating the purpose of your stay, which means providing documents like a job offer, university admission letter, proof of marriage, or client contracts, depending on your visa type. You must also show **proof of financial stability**, whether through bank statements, a job contract with a qualifying salary, a blocked account (commonly used by students or job seekers), or other acceptable financial documents. **Valid health insurance** coverage is essential and must meet German standards; this can be public, private, or travel insurance, depending on your situation. **Proof of accommodation** in Germany—such as a rental agreement or letter from a host—is also typically required. In some cases, especially for family reunification or certain educational programs, **proof of basic German language skills** (usually A1 level) is necessary. Additionally, applicants may be asked to provide a **clean criminal record** from their country of origin. A visa application **fee of €75 (about US$80)** usually applies, although some applicants may be eligible for reduced fees or exemptions.

General Questions

1. *If I want to stay in Germany for long-term and work, should I apply for a work permit before arriving in Germany?*
   Yes. If you're a non-EU or non-EEA citizen and want to work in Germany long-term, you typically need to apply for a work visa before arriving. This national visa (Type D) allows you to enter Germany for employment and is required before you can get a residence permit. You'll need a job offer and must apply through the German embassy or consulate in your home country. After arriving, you register your address and finalize the residence permit with the immigration office. Citizens of countries like the U.S., Canada, or Australia can enter visa-free and apply after arrival, but they can't start working until the permit is approved, so applying in advance is usually the better option.

2. *I am American. Can I retire to Germany?* **Yes.** As an American, you can retire to Germany, though there's no official "retirement visa." Instead, you'd apply for a long-term residence permit for non-working purposes. You'll need to show proof of sufficient income or savings, valid health insurance, and accommodation. The process usually starts with a national visa, followed by applying for the residence permit after arrival. While not guaranteed, many Americans have successfully retired in Germany with the right documentation, especially in quieter, more affordable cities or scenic regions like the Black Forest, Bavaria, or along the Rhine.

 **Law of the Land Hypothetical**

HYPOTHETICAL: *David, a Canadian citizen, has recently been offered a position as a senior consultant with a German company in Munich. He plans to move to Germany alone initially and is wondering if he can bring his partner, Emily, who is also Canadian, to Germany once he settles in. Can David bring his partner, Emily, to Germany, and will Emily be able to work once they are both living there?*

ANSWER: *Yes. David can bring his partner, Emily, to Germany through the **family reunification visa**. Since David will be in Germany on a work visa, Emily can apply for a family reunification visa as his partner. Once approved, she can join him in Germany. Regarding work, Emily may also apply for a work permit after arriving in Germany. Depending on the visa conditions, Emily could be allowed to work without restrictions, particularly if David holds a high-skilled job, or she may need to apply for additional authorization to work. It's important for Emily to check the specific work permit conditions after arrival to ensure she can legally work.*

Law of the Land True Story

Starting January 1, 2025, Germany introduced a **digital platform** for submitting long-term national visa applications, streamlining the process for applicants worldwide, including those from Uzbekistan, Belarus, and the U.S. This shift to online submissions covers 28 visa categories, including work, study, and family reunification visas, but does not include short-term Schengen tourist visas. The new system is designed to expedite visa processing and attract highly skilled professionals to Germany, particularly in response to the growing need for talent in sectors like tourism. By reducing bureaucratic delays, this move modernizes Germany's immigration policies and strengthens its position as a global business hub.

While the online platform is accessible in many countries, some regions like Russia, Ukraine, and Kazakhstan are currently excluded. Applicants can now complete the initial stages of their visa process entirely online, simplifying the application process and enhancing efficiency for both visa seekers and consulates.

Takeaways

- Germany attracts long-term residents with its strong economy, high quality of life, robust healthcare system, low crime rates, and central location in Europe. Major cities like Berlin, Munich, and Hamburg offer unique advantages, while smaller towns provide a slower pace of life and a strong academic or family-friendly environment.

- Germany offers a moderate cost of living, with relatively affordable housing, food, and transportation. Rent can range from €700 – 1,800 (US$745 – 1,915), depending on the city, and public transit is efficient, with options like the Deutschlandticket providing affordable travel across the country.

- The German healthcare system is highly regarded, with mandatory health insurance for all residents. Public health insurance is income-based, and private insurance is available for freelancers or higher earners. This ensures access to quality care across the country.

- While many Germans speak English, learning German is crucial for long-term integration and daily life. Language courses and integration programs are widely available to help expats adapt.

- Germany offers various long-term visa options, including work, student, freelancer, and family reunification visas. These pathways provide clear routes for professionals, students, and families to stay in Germany, with specific requirements based on employment, education, or family status.

CHAPTER 24

CIVIL LITIGATION

CIVIL LITIGATION

Overview

Civil litigation provides a mechanism for resolving disputes, ensuring that travelers have a way to seek justice if legal issues arise while visiting another country. It helps them understand their rights and obligations under local laws, which may differ from those in their home country. The civil litigation system offers a formal process for addressing conflicts, such as contract disputes or personal injury claims, and can deter unfair practices by encouraging businesses to comply with legal standards. It also allows individuals to seek financial recourse for damages or losses and helps protect them from potential exploitation by local entities. Overall, understanding civil litigation enhances a visitor's experience and safety while traveling.

Personal Injury Claims and Compensation Law

In Germany, personal injury claims are primarily governed by civil law, especially the provisions in the **German Civil Code** (*Bürgerliches Gesetzbuch* – BGB). A personal injury claim can be brought when someone suffers harm due to another person's negligence, intentional misconduct, or a legal violation. The most common grounds include traffic accidents, workplace injuries, medical malpractice, and liability for defective products. To establish a valid claim, the injured party must prove that the other person acted unlawfully, that this conduct caused the injury, and that damages resulted from it.

If someone is injured, the first priority is to **seek medical attention**, both for health reasons and to document the injury. The incident should be **reported to the appropriate authorities**—such as the police in case of accidents or assaults—or to the employer if it occurred at work. **Evidence collection** is crucial, including medical reports, witness statements, photos of the scene, and receipts for any related expenses. Once these steps are taken, it's wise to **consult a lawyer** who can assess the legal merits of the case and guide the next actions, especially if compensation is being pursued.

Damages in German personal injury claims are designed to fully **compensate the injured party** for their actual losses, rather than to punish the wrongdoer. This reflects the compensatory nature of German tort law, which does not recognize punitive or exemplary damages, unlike some common law jurisdictions. The primary method used to calculate compensation is the so-called **"difference method,"** which assesses the injured person's economic position before the injury compared to after it. Any financial shortfall resulting from the injury forms the basis of the claim.

Damages are categorized into pecuniary and non-pecuniary types. **Pecuniary damages** cover measurable financial losses such as medical expenses, lost income, costs of rehabilitation, and any future economic disadvantages that can be linked to the injury. **Non-pecuniary damages,** also referred to as *Schmerzensgeld*, compensate for intangible harm like physical pain, emotional suffering, and diminished quality of life. However, it's important to note that awards for pain and suffering in Germany tend to be significantly lower than in countries like the United States.[53]

The amount of compensation awarded depends on several factors, including the severity and permanence of the injury, the extent of lost income or reduced earning capacity, long-term medical needs, and

---

53 https://www.germancivilprocedure.com/checklist-german-tort-claims

whether the injured person contributed to the incident in any way. In cases of contributory negligence, compensation can be reduced proportionally. While there are no rigid statutory caps for most damages, courts often refer to established case law and standardized guidelines to maintain consistency. Additionally, while claimants must normally prove causation and actual loss, German courts have the discretion to estimate damages where precise calculation is difficult, particularly in complex medical or psychological injury cases.

Insurance plays a crucial role in managing both compensation and legal expenses in German personal injury cases. **Liability insurance**, known as *Haftpflichtversicherung*, is the most common form of protection and covers the insured against claims resulting from accidental injury or damage caused to third parties. This type of insurance typically includes coverage for bodily harm, property damage, and associated financial losses. It is a key safeguard, especially in everyday situations where unintentional harm can occur.

In some cases, insurance is not just advisable but **mandatory**. Vehicle owners, for instance, are legally required to carry **motor vehicle liability** insurance, which ensures compensation for third-party injuries or damages in traffic accidents. The same obligation applies to owners of certain large animals, like dogs, and to professionals in high-risk fields such as doctors or architects, where professional liability insurance is a legal or regulatory requirement.[54]

When an incident occurs, the insured party must inform the insurance provider without delay. The insurer then takes over the investigation, determines whether and to what extent liability exists, and may settle claims on behalf of the insured. This includes not only paying out damages but also covering legal defense costs if necessary. In doing so, insurers often resolve matters without court involvement, especially in straightforward traffic or household liability cases.

Court and attorney fees in Germany are **calculated according to the value of the claim** and are governed by statutory fee schedules, meaning

---

54 https://feather-insurance.com/blog/liability-insurance-germany-guide

costs increase with the size and complexity of the case. Germany follows the **"loser pays" principle**, where the losing party is typically required to pay both their own and the opposing party's legal and court fees. The hourly rate of a lawyer in Germany usually varies between **€180 - 500 net** (approximately US$190 - 540). However, there are also lawyers who may agree on rates as low as €100 (around US$110) or as high as €1,000 (about US$1,080), depending on their experience, specialization, and the complexity of the case. However, the German Federal Court of Justice has deemed an hourly rate of **around €290 (approximately US$310)** for legal services to be reasonable.[55] For individuals with low income, **legal aid** (*Prozesskostenhilfe*) can help cover court and attorney fees if the case has merit. Many people also carry legal expenses insurance, which may cover legal representation, court costs, and expert opinions. While contingency or success-based fees are generally prohibited to ensure objectivity and fairness, exceptions are allowed in specific situations where the claimant would not otherwise be able to pursue their case.

How to File a Civil Claim[56]

To initiate a claim, the plaintiff must have a legitimate legal interest and the right to bring the action, meaning they must be **directly affected by the issue**. The claim must also be **timely**, clearly state the facts of the case, and meet any applicable formal or procedural conditions. Most civil claims in Germany are subject to a **general statute of limitations of three years**, starting at the end of the year in which the claimant became aware of the damage and the responsible party.

Civil claims can cover a wide range of issues, including personal injury, breach of contract, property disputes, defamation, and unpaid debts. Smaller claims under **€5,000 (around US$5,400)** are typically handled by the *Amtsgericht* (Local Court), while **higher-value or more complex cases** go to the *Landgericht* (Regional Court). The type of court also

---

55 https://barba-legal.com/en/how-much-does-a-lawyer-cost-in-germany

56 https://www.hilfe-info.de/Webs/hilfeinfo/EN/KnowYourRights/ Zivilprozess/Zivilprozess_node.html)

depends on the nature of the dispute, and specific courts may have exclusive jurisdiction over matters like family law or labor disputes.

To file a civil claim, the claimant must submit a **written complaint** (*Klage*) that includes personal details, a clear explanation of the claim and legal grounds, the requested relief or damages, and supporting evidence. Required documents usually include contracts, correspondence, invoices, medical reports, and any other material relevant to proving the claim. The complaint must be signed and submitted to the competent court in either physical or digital form. Filing fees are also due when the claim is submitted and are calculated based on the claim's value.

The **correct venue for filing** depends on the **defendant's place of residence or registered office**, although exceptions apply in certain cases. For instance, claims related to accidents may also be filed where the incident occurred. Once the court accepts the complaint, it serves it to the defendant, who is then given a deadline to respond, and the formal litigation process begins.

Service of Documents[57]

In Germany, the service of documents in civil proceedings is strictly regulated by the **German Code of Civil Procedure** (*Zivilprozessordnung*) and, in international matters, by the **Hague Service Convention**. These legal rules ensure that all parties in a civil case are properly informed and that the legal process proceeds in a fair and transparent manner. Service of documents is considered an **essential procedural step**, as it officially notifies the recipient of legal action and gives them the opportunity to respond.

Documents are usually served by the **court registry** (*Gerichtsvollzieher*) **ex officio**, meaning the court itself takes responsibility for the process. In certain cases, especially when both parties are represented by legal counsel, documents can also be served by attorneys or via a court bailiff.

---

57   https://maint.loc.gov/law/help/service-of-process/germany.php

The court decides the appropriate method of service, depending on the situation.

There are several ways documents can be served in Germany. **Personal service** at the courthouse is common, particularly for legal representatives. Documents can also be **delivered directly to the recipient** or their authorized representative at home or at work. In some cases, documents are handed to a **qualified third party**, such as a lawyer, notary, tax advisor, or court bailiff. Service can also be completed **through delivery into an official mailbox at court, by messenger, or through certified mail with return receipt**. When personal service is not possible, substituted service is allowed. This means delivery to a household member, a co-worker, or even secure placement in the recipient's mailbox if necessary. For trusted legal professionals and institutions, service may also be done via secure fax or encrypted electronic transmission.

The service process begins once the court or party initiating the case submits the relevant documents for service. The court registry prepares the documents and selects the appropriate delivery method. Once delivered, the recipient—or a substitute recipient—acknowledges receipt, and a formal record of the delivery is created.

Proof of service is always **required**. It is documented either by the postal service (in the case of certified mail) or by the bailiff or authorized individual who carried out the delivery. This documentation includes the date, method, and recipient of the service, and it is returned to the court to be added to the official case file. Without proper service and proof of it, a case cannot move forward, making this step crucial to upholding procedural integrity and the rights of all parties involved.

Statute of Limitations[58]

In Germany, the statute of limitations (*Verjährung*) sets **legal deadlines by which civil claims must be filed**, or they risk becoming unenforceable.

---

58 https://www.ten-law.org/knowledge/
    statute-of-limitation-of-a-legal-claim-under-german-law/

The standard limitation period for most civil claims is three years. This period begins at the end of the calendar year in which the claimant becomes aware—or should have become aware—of the facts that give rise to the claim and the identity of the liable party. For example, if the relevant event occurred in March 2022 and the claimant knew about it at the time, the limitation period would begin on December 31, 2022, and expire on December 31, 2025.

However, different types of claims have **different limitation periods.** Claims related to **personal injury, property damage, or breach of contract** typically follow the standard **three-year rule.** In contrast, claims involving **real property rights** can have a limitation period of **ten years,** and some other cases—like **compensation for intentional torts or damages due to fraud**—may be subject to a limitation period of **up to 30 years.** Employment and tenancy-related disputes may also follow special rules, depending on the specific legal basis.

Several factors can affect how long the statute of limitations lasts. These include the claimant's knowledge of the circumstances, the nature of the claim, and any contractual agreements that may alter the default deadlines. Additionally, certain actions can interrupt or suspend the limitation period. For instance, initiating settlement negotiations, filing a formal claim, or issuing a warning letter can pause the countdown, which then resumes after the interruption ends.

If a civil suit is filed after the applicable statute of limitations has expired, the court will dismiss the claim as **time-barred** if the defendant raises the issue. Once the limitation period has passed, the right to enforce the claim through the courts is lost, even though the underlying obligation may still technically exist.

There are **exceptions** that may extend the statute of limitations. For example, if the claimant was unaware of the harm or the liable party through no fault of their own, the period may be delayed. In cases involving minors or individuals who are mentally incapacitated, the limitation period may not begin until they gain full legal capacity. Force majeure events, such as natural disasters or war, can also suspend the limitation period under certain conditions.

In all cases, knowing and **acting within the limitation period is crucial**, as failing to do so can permanently bar a claim, regardless of its merits.

 ### Getting Married in Germany

Getting married in Germany as a tourist or visitor is legally possible, but it involves **specific requirements** and formal procedures. Both individuals **must be at least 18 years old to marry**. If neither person resides in Germany, the application for marriage must still be submitted to the local registry office, known as the *Standesamt*, in the area where the ceremony is planned. In most cases, at least one party must have been present in Germany for 21 consecutive days before applying. Although some exceptions may apply, depending on the registry office.

To apply for a marriage license, couples must present **valid passports, recent certified copies of their birth certificates** (not older than six months), **a Certificate of No Impediment to Marriage** (*Ehefähigkeitszeugnis*), **proof of legal capacity to marry** (such as a divorce decree or death certificate from a previous spouse, if applicable), and **proof of residence or address in Germany for the required minimum period**. All foreign documents must be officially translated into German and may need to be certified or legalized, depending on the country of origin.

The process of obtaining a marriage license starts with contacting the *Standesamt* to submit all required documents. Once approved, the office schedules a date for the civil ceremony, which must take place within six months of receiving the license. **Only civil ceremonies conducted by the *Standesamt* are legally valid in Germany**. Religious ceremonies may follow but have no legal standing unless preceded by the civil registration.

There are no long-term residency requirements for foreign nationals, but some cities may ask for proof of temporary stay or intent to marry. The entire application process, from submission to marriage, can take several weeks to a few months, depending on how quickly the documents are processed and the availability of appointment slots.

Fees for getting married in Germany typically range from **€50 - 100** (**approximately US$55 - $110**), although this can increase if the ceremony takes place outside the registry office or if translation or notarization services are needed.

Once married, the union is **officially recorded in the German civil registry,** and couples receive a marriage certificate (*Eheurkunde*). This certificate can be used for international legal purposes, such as name changes, visa applications, or spousal benefits. Marriages performed in Germany are **generally recognized internationally,** as long as they comply with both German law and the legal requirements of the other country involved.

 **Law of the Land Hypothetical**

HYPOTHETICAL: *Maria, a Spanish citizen visiting Berlin, is injured when a cyclist runs a red light and crashes into her while she is crossing the street. She suffers a broken arm and incurs medical expenses totaling €4,000 (about US$4,557), along with losing two months of freelance income. The cyclist, a German resident, admits fault at the scene. Can a non-resident like Maria file a personal injury claim in Germany, and what would the process involve?*

ANSWER: *Yes. Maria can file a personal injury claim in Germany as a non-resident. German law allows anyone harmed by another's unlawful actions to seek compensation, and the cyclist's admission of fault gives her a strong basis. She should first file a claim with the cyclist's liability insurer. If unresolved, she can sue in the local court in Berlin where the accident occurred. She'll need to provide evidence like medical bills and proof of lost income. A German lawyer can represent her if she cannot attend. If successful, she may recover damages and legal costs.*

OTHER THINGS TO KNOW

OTHER THINGS TO KNOW

Tourists and Street Hustling

Street hustling and scams in Germany, particularly in tourist-heavy areas, involve various deceptive behaviors aimed at exploiting visitors. **Taxi overcharging** is frequent, particularly when drivers refuse to use the meter or take unnecessarily long routes, especially in cities like Berlin and Stuttgart. **Accommodation scams** are also prevalent, with fake Airbnb or rental listings luring travelers to pay deposits for apartments that don't exist, mainly in Berlin and Munich.

At ATMs, scammers often pose as helpful locals offering assistance but actually use **card skimmers** to steal card details and PINs, leading to unauthorized withdrawals. Another trick involves locals asking tourists to take their photo, then "accidentally" dropping and breaking the camera or phone to extort money or distract them while accomplices pickpocket.

In social settings like bars, friendly locals might encourage groups to order food and drinks but contribute minimally when the bill arrives, leaving tourists to pay the majority. On trains, **fake ticket inspectors** pressure travelers into paying large fines immediately without issuing official penalty notices, unlike legitimate inspectors.

Pickpocketing is common through diversions such as squirting mustard or fake bird droppings on clothing to distract tourists while their belongings are stolen. Similarly, bumping into strangers in crowded places often results in wallets disappearing unnoticed. Beggars sometimes use intimidation or distraction to snatch valuables, and scammers posing as charity workers or friendship bracelet vendors exploit tourists' goodwill to demand money.

These scams are most commonly found in major tourist destinations like Berlin's Mitte district, near landmarks such as the East Side Gallery and Kurfürstendamm. Local authorities and tourism organizations actively address these issues through public awareness campaigns, advising tourists to remain vigilant and report suspicious activities to the police.

To stay safe, tourists should keep valuables secure and be cautious when approached by strangers offering unsolicited assistance or gifts. If targeted by a scam, it's advisable to remain calm, avoid confrontation, and report the incident to local authorities promptly.

To avoid such scams, travelers should insist on using taxi meters, use ATMs inside banks without accepting strangers' help, keep valuables secure, refuse unsolicited offers or gifts, and always ask for official documentation when fined. Staying alert, trusting instincts, and being informed are essential for a safe and enjoyable trip to Germany.

Safety Concerns and Practical Tips

Tourists in Germany should be mindful of safety concerns related to street hustlers, who often use non-violent but aggressive tactics such as pickpocketing, distractions, and scams involving fake fines or services. While physical violence is rare, these hustlers pressure tourists for immediate payments or exploit their trust in crowded places like train stations and markets. To protect themselves, travelers should stay aware of their surroundings, secure valuables in hidden or locked bags, insist on official procedures such as requesting penalty notices from inspectors, and avoid accepting unsolicited help or gifts from strangers. Using reputable transport and accommodations, limiting cash on hand, and being cautious in nightlife areas further reduce risks.

Understanding local behavior can also help. Germans typically maintain personal space and value privacy, so it's perfectly acceptable—and expected—to decline unsolicited interaction with a firm *"Nein, danke"* and keep walking. Eye contact is polite but should not be extended if the interaction feels suspicious.

If a tourist is harassed or falls victim to a scam, they can report the incident to local police (*Polizei*), who are generally helpful and professional. In major cities, many officers speak English. Emergency services can be reached by dialing **110**. Tourist information centers often provide safety tips and may assist in filing reports or directing victims to the proper authorities. Some cities, like Berlin, also offer online police portals where tourists can report non-urgent crimes or scams.

 ## In the Event of Death

If someone traveling with you dies in Germany, the first step is to **contact the local authorities**. If the death occurs in a public place or under suspicious circumstances, you should **call the police at 110**. If the death occurs in a private location, such as a hotel room or hospital, the attending physician must declare the death. The next step is obtaining a **death certificate**, which is issued by the local registry office (*Standesamt*) within three working days.

To handle the deceased's remains, you should **contact a licensed funeral home** (*Bestattungsinstitut*). They will manage the embalming, preparation, and necessary paperwork, including obtaining a medical certificate and an international death certificate. The body must be prepared for repatriation with an **embalming certificate**, a permit from the health authority (*Gesundheitsamt*), and a zinc-lined coffin for transport. If you plan to bring the body home, you'll also need a **transport permit** from the German embassy or consulate.[59]

---

59 da.org/resources/operations-management/shipping-remains

The embassy or consulate of the deceased's home country can assist with documentation, translation services, and coordination with funeral homes. They can also help inform the next of kin. If the deceased had travel or life insurance, it is important to **contact the insurance company** promptly, as they may cover the costs of repatriation and other related expenses. German law requires that all bodies be buried or cremated in designated cemeteries, with alternative burial arrangements subject to strict regulations. Funeral and repatriation costs can be significant, so it's advisable to discuss costs with the funeral home in advance.

It's important to keep multiple copies of all documents, such as the death certificate and identification papers. Staying in communication with the funeral home and embassy throughout the process can help ensure everything is handled efficiently.

Experiencing Financial Hardship

Experiencing financial hardship while traveling in Germany can be distressing, but several resources and strategies can assist tourists in such situations. If you find yourself without funds, the first step is to **contact your home country's embassy or consulate**. They can offer emergency assistance, such as facilitating contact with family or friends, providing information on local charities, or helping with arrangements for funds to be sent. It's advisable to have your passport and any relevant identification available when reaching out. You can also **reach out to your bank or credit card provider** to explore options like emergency cash advances or replacing a lost card. If you've lost all access to money, services like Western Union or MoneyGram allow someone from home to send funds quickly to a local pickup location. Avoid taking loans from unofficial sources and be cautious with anyone offering "quick cash" help on the street. If needed, local police or tourist information offices can point you toward trustworthy services or emergency contacts.

Local support systems include charitable organizations like the **German Red Cross** (*Deutsches Rotes Kreuz*) and **Caritas**, which may provide temporary assistance or direct you to shelters and food services.

Additionally, some cities have emergency funds or low-interest loan programs for travelers in distress.

If you're facing financial hardship, start by assessing how much money you have left and focus only on essentials like food, transport, and accommodation. Shop at discount supermarkets like Aldi or Lidl, eat cheaply from bakeries or cook if you have access to a kitchen. Use public transport with day or weekly passes or walk when possible. For budget accommodations, look into hostels or short-term rentals, and ask local tourist info centers about low-cost options if needed. Use free Wi-Fi in cafés or public places to stay connected. If the situation becomes urgent, contact your embassy. They can guide you or connect you with local support.

QUICK REFERENCE GUIDE

IN THIS CHAPTER

- Quick Chapter References to Important Topics

CHAPTER 26

QUICK REFERENCE GUIDE

Crime in Germany

Are there particular areas I should avoid as a tourist?

Yes. Germany is a very safe country for tourists, but some areas in big cities warrant extra caution, especially at night. Places like Kottbusser Tor in Berlin, the Reeperbahn in Hamburg, or Frankfurt's Bahnhofsviertel can attract petty crime or rowdy crowds. Main train stations late at night and large events like football matches or protests are also worth navigating carefully. Still, most neighborhoods and towns are peaceful, and with basic awareness, your trip should be smooth and enjoyable. *For more details, see Chapter 3.*

Drug Offenses

Is the possession of marijuana legal?

Yes. As of **April 1, 2024, personal possession of cannabis is legal** in small amounts for adults over 18. You're allowed to carry up to **25 grams in public** and keep up to **50 grams at home**. Home cultivation of up to **three plants** is also permitted. However, public consumption is banned near schools, playgrounds, and sports facilities. Commercial sale is still restricted to non-profit "cannabis clubs."

Is the possession of cocaine legal?

> **No. Cocaine is illegal** in Germany under the **Narcotics Act (BtMG)**. Possession, use, sale, or trafficking is a criminal offense and can lead to prosecution, fines, or imprisonment. Even small amounts for personal use are not decriminalized. Though sometimes very small quantities may result in leniency, it's still a criminal matter and not tolerated like cannabis. *For more details, see Chapter 4.*

Alcohol-Related Offenses

What is the legal drinking age?

> The legal drinking age in Germany is **16 for beer, wine, and cider.** However, to purchase or consume **spirits or drinks containing spirits**, you must be **at least 18 years old.** Alcohol consumption is generally not allowed for those under 16 unless under parental supervision in private settings, and even then, spirits are strictly off-limits.

What is the legal blood alcohol limit to drive?

> The legal blood alcohol limit for drivers in Germany is **0.05 percent.** However, there is a **zero-tolerance policy (0.00 percent) for drivers under 21**, those in their probationary period (first two years after getting a license), and professional drivers. Even if you're under the 0.05 percent limit, being involved in an accident or driving unsafely with any alcohol in your system can still lead to legal consequences. *For more details, see Chapter 5.*

Firearm & Ammunition Offenses

Can I possess a gun?

> In Germany, possessing a firearm is strictly regulated. To legally own a gun, you must obtain a weapons possession card, which requires demonstrating a legitimate need, such as for hunting or sport shooting, and passing a background check and competency test. Additionally, you must be **at least 18 years old** and have appropriate

storage arrangements for the firearm. Certain weapons, like fully automatic firearms and pump-action shotguns, are prohibited.

Can I possess ammunition?

To legally possess ammunition in Germany, you need an **ammunition acquisition permit**, which is typically valid for six years. This permit allows you to acquire and possess ammunition for specific types of firearms listed on your weapons possession card. The permit remains effective indefinitely concerning the ownership of the ammunition. Applicants must meet age, reliability, and personal suitability requirements, and demonstrate a legitimate need for the ammunition. *For more details, see Chapter 6.*

Prostitution

Is prostitution legal?

Yes. Prostitution is legal in Germany and regulated by the **Prostitution Act** of 2002. Sex workers have legal rights, including access to health insurance and labor protections. They must register with local authorities and attend health counseling. Brothels are licensed and subject to regulations. However, street prostitution is restricted in many areas and can only occur in designated zones. Soliciting near schools, churches, or residential areas is banned. *For more details, see Chapter 7.*

LGBTQ

Is homosexuality legal?

Yes. Homosexuality is legal in Germany. Same-sex sexual activity was decriminalized in East Germany in 1968 and in West Germany in 1969. Same-sex marriage has been legal nationwide since October 1, 2017, granting same-sex couples full marital and adoption rights.

Are same-sex public displays of affection legal and socially acceptable?

Yes. Same-sex public displays of affection are legal in Germany. German law does not prohibit public affection between same-sex couples. However, public displays of affection that are considered indecent or disruptive to public order can be subject to legal consequences under laws addressing public decency. *For more details, see Chapter 8.*

Arrested in Germany

Would I be entitled to bail if I'm arrested?

In Germany, bail (or *"Kaution"*) is not automatically granted in every case. The decision to grant bail depends on factors like the seriousness of the offense, the risk of flight, and whether there is a risk of tampering with evidence. For less serious offenses, bail may be granted, but for more serious crimes, detention without bail can occur until trial.

Will a lawyer be provided to me if I cannot afford one?

Yes. In Germany, you are entitled to a lawyer, even if you cannot afford one. If you cannot afford to hire a lawyer, a **public defender** (known as a *"Pflichtverteidiger"*) will be appointed to you by the court at no cost. This applies in criminal cases where the potential penalty could involve jail time or other serious consequences. *For more details, see Chapter 10.*

Helping a Friend or Relative Imprisoned in Germany

Can I send money to a friend or relative imprisoned in Germany?

Yes. Inmates are allowed to receive funds, which they can use for things like buying items from the prison canteen, making phone calls, or accessing other allowed services. The usual method is via bank transfer. Each prison typically has a dedicated bank account for inmate funds. It's important to include the inmate's full name and prisoner number in the reference when making the transfer. Before sending money, it's best to contact the specific prison directly to confirm the correct procedure, account details, and any limitations.

Can I remain in the country upon release from prison or jail after my sentence is complete?

Whether you can stay in Germany after serving a sentence depends on your legal status. German citizens can't be deported. EU/EEA citizens can usually stay, though serious crimes might lead to expulsion. Non-EU citizens may face deportation after release, especially for serious or repeated offenses. The immigration authority makes the final decision. *For more details, see Chapter 12.*

Crime Victim Assistance

Can a victim of a crime be legally compensated?

Yes. Victims of crime in Germany can be legally compensated through the **Crime Victims Compensation Act** (*Opferentschädigungsgesetz*). This law provides financial support for victims of violent crimes, including physical injury, psychological harm, or even death. Compensation can cover medical expenses, lost income, and emotional trauma. The government offers this support regardless of whether the offender is caught or able to pay.

Does the German government offer assistance for family members of homicide victims?

Yes. The German government offers assistance to family members of homicide victims. The **Crime Victims Compensation Act** also applies to relatives of victims, providing financial support for funeral expenses, grief counseling, and compensation for psychological harm. In some cases, surviving family members may also be entitled to compensation for loss of income or support. Additionally, there are victim support organizations that offer counseling and legal assistance. *For more details, see Chapter 14.*

U.S. Consulate Assistance

Are there any limitations to the consulate assistance I can receive while in Germany?

Yes. While in Germany, consular assistance is helpful but comes with some limitations. For legal matters, the consulate can help by connecting you with a local lawyer, but it cannot represent you or intervene in the legal process. If you face arrest or legal trouble, they can ensure your rights are upheld but cannot prevent your arrest or affect the outcome. Financially, consulates may offer emergency loans or help you contact family for support, but they generally don't provide long-term financial assistance or pay fines. They also cannot intervene in local jurisdiction, meaning they can't override German law or court decisions. If you lose essential documents, they can issue emergency travel papers, but they can't replace national identity documents. In emergencies like natural disasters, they can assist with evacuation, but they cannot guarantee your safety or provide direct protection. *For more details, see Chapter 14.*

Police

Is there an official police force?

Yes. Germany has an official police force. The primary law enforcement agencies include the **Federal Police** (*Bundespolizei*), which handles federal matters such as border control and transportation security, and the **State Police** (*Landespolizei*), which operates in each of Germany's 16 states and handles general policing duties like patrolling, crime investigation, and maintaining public order. The **Criminal Police** (*Kriminalpolizei*) is a division of the state police focused on investigating serious crimes like murder and theft. These police forces work together and also collaborate with agencies such as the **Federal Criminal Police Office** (*Bundeskriminalamt*) when necessary. *For more details, see Chapter 15.*

How to Get Legal Help in Germany

Is there a resource in Germany to find legal representation?

Yes. In Germany, you can find legal representation through the **German Bar Association** (*Deutscher Anwaltverein*), which has a searchable directory of lawyers. Local courts or municipal offices can also assist in finding a lawyer.

Is there free legal representation assistance?

Yes. There is some free legal representation assistance available in Germany. If you're unable to afford a lawyer, you may be eligible for **legal aid** (*Prozesskostenhilfe*), which covers the cost of legal representation for those with limited income. This aid is available for both criminal and civil cases, though you may need to meet certain financial criteria to qualify.

Does my home country's embassy provide a list of local attorneys that speak my native language?

Yes. Your home country's embassy or consulate in Germany typically provides a list of local attorneys who speak your language. They can give you referrals or point you to local legal resources, but they don't offer direct legal services. The embassy can help connect you with local lawyers, ensuring you have access to proper representation in legal matters. *For more details, see Chapter 16.*

Foreign Embassies in Germany

Are there foreign embassies in Germany?

Yes. There are foreign embassies in Germany. Many countries have embassies in Berlin, and consulates in other major cities like Frankfurt, Munich, and Hamburg, providing consular services such as visa issuance, legal assistance, and emergency support for their citizens.

Is there a website to locate embassies in Germany?

Yes. To locate embassies in Germany, you can visit the **German Foreign Office** (*Auswärtiges Amt*) website at **www.auswaertiges-amt.de/en/about-us/auslandsvertretungen**. This platform provides a comprehensive list of foreign embassies, consulates, and their contact information in Germany. *For more details, see Chapter 16.*

Medical Facilities & Hospitals

Is there a number I can call for ambulance and fire emergencies?

Yes. In Germany, the emergency number for both **ambulance** and **fire emergencies** is **112**. This number works throughout the country and connects you to emergency services for medical, fire, or rescue situations.

If I am injured while on vacation in Germany, are there hospitals that are recommended for tourists?

Yes. If you're injured while on vacation in Germany, most cities have **public and private hospitals** that are equipped to handle emergencies. Some well-regarded hospitals for tourists include **Charité University Hospital** in Berlin, **University Hospital Munich** (LMU), and **St. Joseph Hospital** in Hamburg. These hospitals are known for their high-quality care, and many have English-speaking staff, making them more accessible for international visitors. It's recommended to check if your travel insurance covers emergency medical services before seeking treatment. *For more details, see Chapter 17.*

Driving in Germany

Which side of the road do I drive on?

In Germany, you drive on the **right side of the road.**

Can I use my driver's license from my home country to drive in Germany?

Yes. You can use your driver's license from your home country to drive in Germany, especially for short visits (**up to six months**). If you're staying longer or become a resident, you may need to exchange it for a German license, depending on your country of origin.

How old do I need to be to rent a car?

> To **rent a car** in Germany, you typically need to be **at least 21 years old**, though this can vary by rental company. Some companies may charge an extra fee for drivers under 25, and in some cases, the minimum age may be higher for certain types of vehicles. *For more details, see Chapter 18.*

Nude Beaches & Clothing-Optional Resorts

Is public nudity legal on the beaches?

> **Yes**. Public nudity is generally legal on certain beaches in Germany, especially in designated **FKK** (*Freikörperkultur*) areas, which are popular for naturism. While nudity is accepted and legal in these designated zones, it's important to respect local customs, as public nudity outside these areas (like in towns or more private locations) may be considered inappropriate and subject to fines. So, always look for signs or check the specific rules of the beach you're visiting. *For more details, see Chapter 19.*

Tourist Taxation

Is there room tax in Germany?

> **Yes. Room tax** (also known as **tourism tax** or **city tax**) exists in many parts of Germany, especially in popular tourist destinations. The tax is typically a small percentage of the accommodation cost and is usually paid directly to the hotel or accommodation provider. Rates vary depending on the location.

Is there any fee associated with leaving Germany?

> There is **no specific fee for leaving the country**, whether by air, land, or sea. However, if you're flying, you may encounter taxes or fees included in the cost of your plane ticket, such as airport security charges or international departure fees, but these are generally included in your ticket price rather than being paid separately when leaving. *For more details, see Chapter 22.*

Long-Term Stays

As an American, do I need to return to my home country to apply for a work permit in Germany?

> **No.** As an American, you **do not need to return to your home country** to apply for a work permit in Germany. You can apply for a German work visa or residence permit while you are in Germany. However, you cannot begin working until your permit is granted. The process can involve gathering required documents, such as proof of employment, qualifications, and financial means.

As an American, how long can I stay in Germany without a visa?

> As an American citizen, you can stay in Germany for up to **90 days within a 180-day period** for tourism, business, or family visits under the Schengen Agreement. However, if you plan to stay longer or work, you will need to apply for the appropriate visa or residence permit. *For more details, see Chapter 23.*

In the Event of Death

What documents would an embassy need regarding the death of a tourist?

> When a tourist dies abroad, an embassy typically requires the **death certificate** issued by local authorities to confirm the death, along with the **deceased's passport** to verify their identity and nationality. Proof of death from local authorities, such as a police or medical report, may be necessary if the death was due to unnatural causes. Documentation showing the relationship of the next of kin, like a marriage or birth certificate, is important, as is **any travel insurance information.** Flight details may be needed for repatriation of the body, and if the death involved an accident or crime, a police or investigation report might be required. These documents help the embassy assist with repatriation, notifying family, and handling legal matters. *For more details, see Chapter 25.*

EMERGENCY/IMPORTANT CONTACT NUMBERS IN GERMANY

 Please consider putting some of these numbers in your phone **prior** to traveling to Germany.

Emergency Numbers:

- **Police:** 110
- **Fire:** 112
- **Ambulance:** 112

Other Useful Contacts:

- **General Emergency Services:** 112
- **Tourist Police:** 110
- **Coast Guard:** +49 421 53 6870 or +49 (0) 4631 6013
- **Roadside Assistance:** 110

Legal Assistance:

- **German Bar Association:** + 49 (0) 30 284 9390
- **Legal Aid:** +49 30 83050

USEFUL GERMAN PHRASES

Greetings

HI/HELLO – Hallo

GOOD MORNING – Guten Morgen

GOOD AFTERNOON – Guten Tag

GOOD NIGHT – Gute Nacht

GOODBYE – Auf Wiedersehen

Magic Words

PLEASE – Bitte

THANK YOU – Danke

YOU'RE WELCOME – Gern geschehen

CHEERS! – Prost!

EXCUSE ME – Entschuldigung

Getting Around

WHERE IS THE BATHROOM? – Wo befindet sich das Badezimmer?

WHAT TIME IS IT? – Wie spät ist es?

HOW DO I GET TO...? – Wie komme ich zu...?

WHERE DOES THIS TRAIN/BUS GO? – Wohin fährt dieser Zug/Bus?

RESTAURANT – Restaurant

HOW MUCH DOES THIS COST? – Wie viel kostet das?

TRAIN/METRO STATION – Bahnhof/U-Bahn-Station

Communication

DO YOU SPEAK ENGLISH? – Sprechen Sie Englisch?

I DO NOT UNDERSTAND – Ich kann Sie nicht verstehen

I DON'T SPEAK GERMAN – Ich spreche kein Deutsch

I DON'T KNOW – Ich weiß es nicht

Emergency

HELP! – Hilfe!

CALL AN AMBULANCE! – Rufen Sie einen Krankenwagen!

I NEED A DOCTOR – Ich benötige einen Arzt

POLICE – Polizei

I'M LOST – Ich habe mich verlaufen

IT'S AN EMERGENCY – Es ist ein Notfall

GLOSSARY

ACQUITTAL: A jury verdict that a criminal defendant is not guilty, or the finding of a judge that the evidence cannot support a conviction.

ADVERSARY PROCEEDING: A lawsuit arising from a controversy that begins with filing a complaint.

AFFIDAVIT: A written statement made under oath.

APPEAL: A request made after a trial court has decided against one party in which the losing party asks a higher court to review the decision for legal error.

ARRAIGNMENT: A proceeding in which a criminal defendant is brought to court, told of the charges, and asked to plead guilty or not guilty.

BAIL: The temporary release of a person from jail when awaiting trial, on condition that a sum of money be lodged or deposited to guarantee an appearance in court.

BARRISTER: A lawyer admitted to plead at the Bar and who may try cases in superior court.

BURDEN OF PROOF: The duty to prove disputed facts.

CAUSE OF ACTION: A legal claim in a civil action.

COMPLAINT: A written statement that begins a civil lawsuit in which the plaintiff details the claims.

CONTRACT: An agreement between two or more persons to do something or to not do something.

CONVICTION: A judgment of guilt against a person charged with a crime.

CUSTOMS DUTY: A tariff or tax imposed on goods when transported across international borders.

COURT LIAISON: A person that coordinates with attorneys to perform administrative duties, such as scheduling witnesses, sharing information with law enforcement, and overseeing the reporting of cases to foreign embassies when applicable.

DAMAGES: Money that a defendant pays to a plaintiff in a civil case if the plaintiff wins.

DEFENDANT: 1) The individual against whom a civil claim is filed; 2) The individual against whom a criminal claim is filed.

FELONY: A serious crime, punishable by more than one year in prison.

MAGISTRATE: A judicial officer of a district court, who conducts initial proceedings in criminal cases, decides criminal misdemeanor cases, conducts many pretrial civil and criminal matters on behalf of district judges, and decides civil cases with the consent of the parties.

MISDEMEANOR: An offense punishable by one year or less in jail.

PLAINTIFF: A person or business that files a formal complaint with the court.

PLEA: In a criminal case, the answer of "guilty," "not guilty," or "no contest" in response to a criminal charge.

SOLICITOR: A lawyer who advises clients, represents them in lower court, and prepares cases for barristers to try in higher courts.

SOVEREIGN IMMUNITY: A legal doctrine by which the sovereign or the state (i.e. government) cannot commit a legal wrong and thus, it is immune from criminal and civil liability and cannot be sued.

STATUTE: A written law passed by a legislative body.

STATUTE OF LIMITATIONS: A statute prescribing a period of limitation to bring certain types of legal actions. If the action is not brought within that time, the person or entity (in a criminal context) is permanently barred from suing in court.

SUBPOENA: A command, issued under court authority, for a witness to appear and to give testimony.

TESTIMONY: Evidence presented orally by witnesses.

VERDICT: The decision of a judge or jury in a case.

WARRANT: Court authorization to conduct a search or to make an arrest.

ACKNOWLEDGMENTS

This book series would never have seen the light of day without the able assistance of the following people:

Kathy Adams, my paralegal for over 22 years, who is the "Best" I've ever worked with during my entire legal career because of her amazing work ethic, organizational skills, and her ability to think outside of the box in unique and creative ways;

Ally Knez-Siddique, a professional writer, and one of my paralegals, whose eye for detail, according to her, is both a blessing and a curse;

Gino Ibanez, my former law clerk, whose exceptional research skills helped move this book series along in its early stages;

Rosa Diaz Graham, my legal assistant who helped with research and word processing at the very beginning of this project;

Shelia Martin, one of my former paralegals, worked diligently on this series of books, even after taking on another job. Her organizational skills are reflected throughout;

Oliver Clark, whose hard work and diligence researching and writing, helped bring this book to life.

Mindy Scarlett, my marketing and publishing "Guru"! Her creativity and vision have no boundaries!

ABOUT THE AUTHOR

Michael L. Moore practices in Orlando, Florida, the city where he spent his formative years. He credits the trauma of having his brother murdered when he was only 10 years old, as the catalyst that drew him into the practice of law.

Moore attended Florida State University, where he was a member of the FSU debate team. Upon graduating, he was awarded a full scholarship to attend the University of Tennessee College of Law, where he was elected President of the Student Bar Association. He further honed his advocacy and public speaking skills by participating in 'moot court' competitions.

After clerking at the Tennessee Attorney General's office while in law school, Moore moved back to Orlando, Florida, to work at the State Attorney's Office as a prosecutor, and where he was fortunate enough to meet the young lady that would eventually become his wife. Moore moved on to working for private law firms, both local and national, and eventually established his own law firm in 1999. He continues to make Orlando his home base.

It was the murder of a close friend and client in Jamaica that caused Moore to realize that books on laws in other countries were few and far between, and he was inspired to create Law of the Land Publishing. Moore launched Law of the Land Publishing to provide a series of guidebooks and a membership site for tourists and business travelers to stay up to date on the laws in each country they travel to, as well as having access to assistance if they run into legal issues.

"My vision is to educate people on what their legal rights are, and how they can access legal assistance, no matter where they have to travel to in the world," said Moore. "As Americans, we have a right to due process, but in some countries, you don't even have the right to access a square meal when incarcerated. My goal is to provide the information needed to stay out of trouble, as well as having access to assistance if trouble finds you."

www.ingramcontent.com/pod-product-compliance
Lightning Source LLC
Chambersburg PA
CBHW070915120626
46546CB00001B/273